What people are saying about *A Divine Revelation of Angels* and Mary Baxter's Ministry

The Bible frequently mentions angels—God's heavenly messengers or servants. In *A Divine Revelation of Angels,* Mary Baxter combines biblical teaching with her own experiences, giving the reader thought-provoking and enlightening insights about the ministry of angels.

Dr. David Yonggi Cho
Senior Pastor, Yoido Full Gospel Church
Seoul, Korea

A Divine Revelation of Angels describes the dreams, revelations, and visions of Mary Baxter, revealing angels at work today. It is most interesting and absorbing. I believe you will be inspired by this book.

Oral Roberts
Founder and Chancellor, Oral Roberts University
Tulsa, Oklahoma

Mary Baxter's previous works have earned her thousands of fans all over the world. In *A Divine Revelation of Angels,* she tells of her own experiences with angels and makes a case for these heavenly beings at work in our lives. God cares enough about us to send us extra help in those special times when our strength alone is insufficient. You will be blessed by her work.

Dr. Bill George
Editor in Chief, Church of God Publications
Cleveland, Tennessee

Author Mary Baxter takes us on a journey that reminds us of how much God really cares for us and watches over us. This book about angels is filled with her experiences in dreams and visions from God, but what she says is backed up by Scripture. You will rejoice in your spirit as you read about the miraculous and unusual ways God rescues and provides for His children. God is speaking to us through these words.

Jentezen Franklin
Pastor, Free Chapel Worship Center
Kingdom Connection Int'l Television Program
Gainesville, Georgia

Through the years, Mary Baxter has captured the imagination of the body of Christ and directed it heavenward. Her new book with Dr. T. L. Lowery, *A Divine Revelation of Angels,* takes us higher yet anchors our feet in solid doctrinal ground.

John A. Kilpatrick
Senior Pastor, Brownsville Assembly of God
Pensacola, Florida

The work of angels, God's messengers, can be seen throughout Scripture. However, many believers today have a man-created vision of angels. Who they are and what they do are often misunderstood due to the work of the secular press and its influence over television, film, and popular literature. *A Divine Revelation of Angels* sets the record straight! A book that is both scripturally sound and easy for anyone to understand.

Rod Parsley
Pastor, World Harvest Church
CEO, Breakthrough Media Ministries
Columbus, Ohio

Mary K. Baxter's books have reached around this world and have impacted people in all walks of life. As people get the opportunity to meet her and witness the power of God on her life, they learn it truly is *A Divine Revelation* from God." —*T. L. Gabbard, Sr., Pastor, Wynne, Arkansas*

We have been blessed by Mary Baxter's ministry at our church....Hundreds have been saved and filled with the Holy Spirit, and many have been healed and set free. —*Winford Walters, Pastor, Elyria, Ohio*

Mary Baxter has been a great blessing to our church family. Through her preaching abilities, many people have gotten saved and delivered, and a great number of backsliders have rededicated their lives back to God.... I believe that her written testimonies will change the lives of countless unbelievers and strengthen the faith of many believers concerning heaven and hell. —*Jason Alvarez, Pastor, Orange, NJ*

Mary Baxter has preached at our church many times, and lots of people were saved and healed....Her ministry has touched many lives in the kingdom of God. —*Gladys Boggs, pastor's wife, Houston, Texas*

Mary Baxter truly has an incredible testimony that needs to be shared with all. God surely is using Mary as a soul winner for Jesus Christ. —*Eldred Thomas, President, KLTJ–TV, Houston, Texas*

I wish [Mary's] book[s] could be made available to everyone—to Christians as a warning to continue walking with Jesus, and to non-Christians to show them what is awaiting them if they do not commit their lives to Jesus Christ. *R. Russell Bixler, Founder, Cornerstone TV, Wall, Pennsylvania*

To give praise, honor, and glory
to God, this book is dedicated to
The Father,
The Son,
and
The Holy Spirit

A DIVINE REVELATION *of* ANGELS

MARY K. BAXTER
with Dr. T. L. Lowery

WHITAKER
HOUSE

A DIVINE REVELATION OF ANGELS

For speaking engagements, please contact:

Evangelist Mary K. Baxter   Lowery Ministries International
Divine Revelation, Inc.   P. O. Box 2550
www.mbaxterdivinerevelation.org   Cleveland, TN 37320-2550

ISBN-13: 978-0-88368-866-3
ISBN-10: 0-88368-866-2
Printed in the United States of America
© 2003 by Lowery Ministries International

Whitaker House
1030 Hunt Valley Circle
New Kensington, PA 15068
www.whitakerhouse.com

Library of Congress Cataloging-in-Publication Data

Baxter, Mary K.
   A divine revelation of angels / Mary K. Baxter with T. L. Lowery.
      p. cm.
   ISBN 0-88368-866-2
   1. Angels. 2. Private revelations. I. Lowery, T. L. (Thomas Lanier),
1929– II. Title.
   BT966.3.B39 2003
   235'.3—dc21
                                      2003008414

6 7 8 9 10 11 12 **UJ** 15 14 13 12 11 10

Contents

Foreword

Sir Francis Bacon said,

Some books are to be tasted, others to be swallowed, and some few to be chewed and digested: that is, some books are to be read only in parts, others to be read, but not curiously, and some few to be read wholly, and with diligence and attention.

This is one of those books to be chewed and digested. It is to be studied and enjoyed. Its subject matter may at times be controversial, but the study of angels is of great importance in this day and age. The topic of angels is not a new one, yet it is current and relevant. There is much confusion about angels, and therefore much misinformation is being circulated about these heavenly beings. I believe it is vital that we know what the Bible, the great Word of God, has to say about this most important subject.

Mary Katherine Baxter is a choice servant of God. She is anointed and boldly fearless in her proclamation of the truth of God's Word. In these last days, the sovereign Lord has especially chosen her to receive marvelous and breathtaking revelations that give all of us amazing light on spiritual matters.

Her first book describing her divine revelations, *A Divine Revelation of Hell*, is an eyewitness account of what she saw taking place among the lost souls who refuse to believe and end up in hell.

A Divine Revelation of Heaven, her second book, describes the beauties and rewards that God permitted her to see so that she could "tell others about that wonderful place."

Her third book, *A Divine Revelation of the Spirit Realm*, is a treasure chest of resource and encouragement for those who are engaged in spiritual warfare.

This latest volume, *A Divine Revelation of Angels*, does two things. First, it presents the believer with a study of angels; it tells what the Bible has to say about them. Again, with all the misinformation and erroneous teaching about angels today, it is important that God's truth be known. I have collaborated with Mary Baxter in the writing of this book. We have searched the Scriptures diligently, and we present this material with the assurance that its teachings are backed up by the Bible. This book is solidly biblical.

Second, this book relates faithfully the visions and revelations that God has given to Mary

Baxter concerning angels. What she writes and describes speaks to the heart about these spiritual, heavenly creatures.

This series of books has already blessed hundreds of thousands of people in many countries. The wide acceptance of these writings and the enthusiastic feedback from people whose lives have been changed by the reading of them is gratifying, indeed.

My prayer for you is that God will bless you and keep you. May He cause His face to shine on you, and may He bless you in everything you do. I pray that God will give you a fresh anointing and renewed vision as you read this book, so that you may be abundantly fruitful in building His kingdom and participating in the end-times harvest.

—Dr. T. L. Lowery

Introduction

his book explores what the Bible says about angels. It is also a true account of the many experiences God has given to me concerning His heavenly messengers. I know that God has promised,

> *Because you have made the LORD, who is my refuge, even the Most High, your dwelling place, no evil shall befall you, nor shall any plague come near your dwelling; for He shall give His angels charge over you, to keep you in all your ways. In their hands they shall bear you up.*
> (Psalm 91:9–12)

I believe the angels were with me in the writing of this book. Also, many people helped to make this project possible. I want to acknowledge a few of them.

First, I want to thank my pastor, mentor, and spiritual advisor, the Reverend Dr. T. L. Lowery, for his invaluable assistance. Without him and his advice, prayer, and help, this book would not and could not have been written. I honor him and his beautiful wife, Mildred, for their support, encouragement, and valuable assistance in this ministry.

I sincerely thank my church, the National Church of God in Washington, D.C., and my pastor, the Reverend Stephen Lowery, for their support and encouragement.

I gratefully recognize and credit those at Whitaker House in New Kensington, Pennsylvania, who have been so instrumental in making these messages from God available to the reading public.

Most of all, I am grateful to God who has called me to share these messages. I give all praise and honor and glory to God the Father, God the Son, and God the Holy Spirit.

—Mary K. Baxter

Part I

The Nature of Angels

I

Are Angels Real?

eople have been captivated by the idea of angels for centuries. Throughout history, most religions have held certain beliefs concerning spiritual beings, powers, and principalities. In ancient times, unenlightened pagans usually believed spiritual beings were the disembodied spirits of departed ancestors, spirits of things in nature, or fairy beings from another world.

Archaeologists have discovered representations of winged beings in early cave art, etched on walls and cliffs. The classical artists of the medieval period popularized the use of artistic symbols in their works, so that one could immediately recognize an angel in a painting. They usually showed angels as humanlike figures with wings, white robes, halos, and often harps or other types of musical instruments. The wings on the angels were meant to signify that they were celestial beings. Their white robes and halos symbolized

17

purity and holiness. The musical instruments were included to indicate that angels sing praises to God. Depictions of angels in both medieval and Renaissance paintings contribute to many of our current ideas about what angelic beings look and act like.

"Angel Mania"

Angels are a hugely popular subject in today's society. In my ministry travels over the past few years, I have observed a steadily rising interest in celestial beings among people of all walks of life. Everywhere I go, people ask me about angels. Even Christians from more traditional backgrounds that don't usually emphasize the supernatural realm show an increasing fascination with these heavenly creatures.

There are many signs of a widespread interest in angels not only in the church, but also throughout our society. Our museums are crammed full of paintings and sculptures of winged beings. Best-seller lists regularly feature titles about angels. Bookstores have whole sections of their displays devoted to celestial beings.

In addition, we regularly read and see reports in the media about angels. A current popular television show called *Touched by an Angel* suggests the existence of guardian angels. Not long ago, another highly rated program called *Highway to*

Heaven featured an angel sent to earth to assist mortals.

The lyrics of many popular songs speak about angels. Representations of celestial beings also appear on birthday cards and wedding invitations. They abound as souvenirs, jewelry, and religious or semi-religious dust catchers. Artists and writers continue to depict angels in many forms.

Time magazine published a cover story entitled "Angels among Us." The writers of the article explained the phenomenon of the current craze for angels in this way:

> For those who choke too easily on God and his rules, theologians observe, angels are the handy compromise, all fluff and meringue, kind, nonjudgmental. And they are available to everyone, like aspirin.

It seems that many people today use the idea of angels to ease their consciences, escape the realities of life, and enter an imaginary world that seems pleasant and nondemanding.

What are angels? Do such creatures really exist? Or are they make-believe, like elves and fairies? Are they just beings that fertile minds have conjured up, imaginary figures that have become hopelessly suspended between reality and fantasy? If they do exist, how can we be sure? Can they be seen?

My Interest in Angels

My own interest in angels is more than a passing fad or craze. Many years ago, God began to give me dreams, visions, and revelations of the spiritual realm, including those that revealed the work of His angels. I am not referring to special people who are "angels" to us; I am talking about God's spirit messengers, His special agents who do His bidding and are sent to rescue His people. These visions and revelations usually came when I was in prayer and meditation on God's Word.

I have written about many of these experiences in my books *A Divine Revelation of Hell, A Divine Revelation of Heaven,* and *A Divine Revelation of the Spirit Realm.** In these accounts, I tell in great detail of the revelation knowledge God has given to me and what He has shown me over the years concerning His mysteries. In *A Divine Revelation of Angels,* I want to emphasize the visions and revelations of angels that God has given to me. I want to show what the work of angels in our lives means for us as we love and serve God.

In 1976, when I started telling the story of the revelations God had given to me, I was like a pioneer pushing into unfamiliar territory. When I went out to speak, there were times when I was mocked, persecuted, and ridiculed. But I kept

* published by Whitaker House

20

telling my story because I felt I had a mandate from God. Today, God is sending manifestations and revelations in abundance. God has mysteries to reveal to us at this hour, and we must believe Him.

The Purpose of God's Revelations

I am Christ's servant, and I'm excited about the fact that He is merciful and good to His servants. God has given me these visions and revelations so that, in turn, I can give them to the body of Christ and to those who are not yet believers. They are signs that God is working among us. The Bible says, *"Surely the Lord GOD does nothing, unless He reveals His secret to His servants the prophets"* (Amos 3:7). God has revealed these things to give us hope, to encourage us, and to show us that He is with us.

What I will relate to you lines up with the Word of God. I know from the Bible and from the revelations God has given me that angels—real angels—are not myths or legends. They are more than a marketing gimmick or a premise for a television program. They are true spiritual beings.

I write these things to lift up Jesus Christ, to exalt Him. The purpose of these revelations is to draw people close to God and to bring Him honor and glory. You need to know just how much Jesus loves and cares about you. There is so much He wants to talk to you about, so much

He wants to open up your heart to. He desires your companionship. He desires to reveal Himself to you. You can talk to Him, and He will talk to you. He is an awesome, loving God!

I want you to know that I love the Lord Jesus with all my heart. He is so good to me. What I'm saying in this book is true. I want you to understand this so that you can sit with Christ in heavenly places. This is something He wants for all of us:

> *But God, who is rich in mercy, because of His great love with which He loved us, even when we were dead in trespasses, made us alive together with Christ (by grace you have been saved), and raised us up together, and made us sit together in the heavenly places in Christ Jesus.*
> (Ephesians 2:4–6)

God has put it on my heart to write this book about angels. He is inspiring books to be written to let the world know what a good God He is and how He takes care of His people. I've seen angels in action many times, and I'm praying that the Holy Spirit will guide me as I relate some of these revelations to you. As I write down what God has given me to share, I pray that it will strengthen and enlighten you in the mysteries and revelations of God.

I also pray that this book will go all over the world to help many other people who need

God—that these testimonies of angels in action will help thousands of people know the reality of God's love and concern for them. Through the truths presented here, I'm praying that God— either directly or through His angels—will undo heavy burdens, heal sicknesses and diseases in the name of Jesus, and help the oppressed go free. It is God's desire *"to loose the bonds of wickedness, to undo the heavy burdens, to let the oppressed go free, and...break every yoke"* (Isaiah 58:6).

I get excited all over again when I remember the marvelous revelations God has given me and what He has shown me about His holy angels. Truly God has mercy, and He has angels working for our benefit. In Parts I and II of this book, I will explain what the Bible has to say about the nature and role of angels. In Part III, I will relate what the Lord has revealed to me by His Holy Spirit about these heavenly messengers. I will also share some visions I've seen of the angels of God in action. These visions emphasize the many ways that angels bring glory to God and carry out His commands to guide, protect, comfort, defend, and deliver His people. Part IV provides an opportunity for personal reflection or group discussion of the themes presented in each chapter.

In the next chapter, we will learn what is true and what is myth concerning God's heavenly messengers.

2

The Truth about Angels

The study of angels is a serious and sacred pursuit. You have to be careful about some of the teachings you hear and read on the subject, especially what you find on the Internet. Much of so-called teaching on angels making the rounds these days—even in religious circles—is false, and it causes people to be deceived. In this day when we are experiencing a wave of "angel mania," it is important to know what God's Word says about angels. Uninformed conceptions of angels abound, as they have in the past, but I am writing these pages to declare the truth! The things I describe in this book are reality; none of them is fantasy.

Good and Evil Angels

Many people do not realize that there are *two* kinds of angels operating in the world today. This is why people can often become confused and deceived about the nature and role of celestial beings. Not all angels are kind and benevolent. There are good angels and there are evil angels.

Good angels continually seek to do God's will, and they work for our benefit. Evil angels seek to deceive us about their true intentions toward us. They are demons who want to harm us rather than help us. This is why it can be very dangerous to learn about angels from those who don't have a solid biblical understanding of their true nature and ways. I believe that one reason God wanted me to write this book was so people could know how to tell the difference between angels who want to help them and angels who desire to harm them. In this book, I mainly describe the things God has revealed to me concerning His good angels. We have to understand the truth about God's holy angels if we are going to be able to discern what is counterfeit.

Angels in the Bible

Angels have been written about prominently in the Scriptures, and the Bible teaches that they are real beings. The Bible is our best source for understanding the true nature of angels because it is God's own Word. *"Every word of God is flawless"* (Proverbs 30:5 NIV).

In the Scriptures, the words *angel* and *angels* appear about three hundred times (combined), and the work of angels is referred to almost two hundred fifty times. Angels are mentioned in thirty-four books of the Bible (a little over half the books). The Hebrew word for angel most commonly used in the Old Testament is *mal'ak*, and the Greek word for angel most frequently used in the New Testament is *aggelos*. Both of these words mean "a messenger." (See *Strong's* #G32; #H4397.)

Scripture makes reference to the origin of angels and various types of angels, and it reveals important facts about their character, habits, and actions—much of which are contrary to popular belief about angels today. I will talk more about the nature and ways of angels in the next chapter. However, we must first recognize the following truths about angels in order to understand who they are and how they work in our lives.

Angels Were Created

First, what is the origin of angels? Did they always exist?

The Bible tells us that angels are a company of spiritual beings that were created by God Himself. For example, in the Old Testament, we read,

> *Praise* [the Lord], *all His angels; praise Him, all His hosts!...Let them praise the name of the LORD, for He commanded and they were created.* (Psalm 148:2, 5)

In the New Testament, we find,

> *All things were made through Him, and without Him nothing was made that was made.* (John 1:3)

> *By* [Jesus] *all things were created that are in heaven and that are on earth, visible*

27

*and invisible, whether thrones or domin-
ions or principalities or powers. All things
were created through Him and for Him.*
(Colossians 1:16)

There is nothing anywhere that God did not
create, including the angels.

The Bible doesn't tell us exactly when angels
were created, but it indicates that they already
existed and were present when God created the
earth. God asked Job,

*Where were you when I laid the earth's
foundation? Tell me, if you understand.
Who marked off its dimensions? Surely
you know! Who stretched a measuring
line across it? On what were its footings
set, or who laid its cornerstone—while
the morning stars sang together **and all
the angels shouted for joy**?*
(Job 38:4–7 NIV, emphasis added)

Angels Are Not Gods

Second, many people today think that angels
are divine, and they look to them for direction in
life. I have seen some books advertised that pur-
port to tell you how to contact "your" angel. Some
who present themselves as experts on angels tell
their followers to love their angels and call upon
them for health, healing, prosperity, and guidance.

This teaching is contrary to God's Word.
Angels are neither our gods nor our direct

spiritual guides. They are not available for use at our convenience, like aspirin. They are not genies that we can summon to fulfill our wishes. We cannot call down an angel any time we want to, just by repeating certain phrases or reciting a magic formula or mantra. Angels are God's servants, not ours. They come and go at His bidding. They respond to His voice, not to our commands or requests:

> *Bless the LORD, you His angels, who excel in strength, who do His word, heeding the voice of His word. Bless the LORD, all you His hosts, you ministers of His, who do His pleasure.* (Psalm 103:20–21)

We are never to pray to angels or to call on angels for guidance or deliverance. We are to pray only to the Lord Himself. Praying to an angel may open you up to spiritual deception, especially if you are a new Christian or are not walking close to God. You won't be able to spiritually discern the true nature of an encounter with an angel. When you talk to a being that appears or claims to be an angel, you may be talking to a deceiving spirit masquerading as an angel of light. (See 2 Corinthians 11:14.)

However, when you talk to Jesus, you never go wrong. When you ask God to guide or deliver you, He may use an angel to help you. Yet make no mistake—it is God who is delivering you, even though He may do so *through* His angels.

It is God whom we are to trust, not angels. The Bible doesn't tell us to love angels; it tells us to love God (Matthew 22:37). All the attention, emphasis, and glory should go to God, not to His servants! God Himself says, *"My glory I will not give to another"* (Isaiah 42:8).

As great as angels are, therefore, we are never to worship them. False teachers will draw you into the worship of angels, which will lead you away from God's truth and into deception. The Bible warns us about this:

> *Let no one cheat you of your reward, taking delight in false humility and worship of angels, intruding into those things which he has not seen, vainly puffed up by his fleshly mind, and not holding fast to* [Christ].   (Colossians 2:18–19)

We should respect angels, admire their dedication to God, and appreciate their ministries to God and to us, but we are forbidden to worship them.

One thing I have noticed about real encounters with angels is that God's holy angels never bring attention to themselves. They usually just do their work quietly, often behind the scenes and unnoticed, and they leave when the work is done. Their lives and actions are always consistent with the character of Christ. They always glorify God, not themselves. Therefore, a true angel of God will not accept worship from a human being.

Instead, he will always tell you to worship God. In Revelation 19, the apostle John wrote that when he encountered an angel, he was so awed that he *"fell at his feet to worship him"* (v. 10). However, the angel told John,

See that you do not do that! I am your fellow servant, and of your brethren who have the testimony of Jesus. Worship God! For the testimony of Jesus is the spirit of prophecy. (v. 10)

Again, in Revelation 22, John wrote,

Now I, John, saw and heard these things. And when I heard and saw, I fell down to worship before the feet of the angel who showed me these things. Then he said to me, "See that you do not do that. For I am your fellow servant, and of your brethren the prophets, and of those who keep the words of this book. Worship God." (vv. 8–9)

Angels are fellow servants and co-worshipers of God with human beings. In his vision of heaven, John saw all the angels giving glory, honor, and praise to the One who sits on the throne. (See Revelation 5:13; 7:11–12.) He described heavenly beings praising God and exalting Him with the words, *"Holy, holy, holy, Lord God Almighty, who was and is and is to come!"* (Revelation 4:8). He saw the twenty-four elders fall down in worship and cast their crowns before the throne. (See verses 9–10.) Then he heard their shouts of praise: *"You are worthy, O Lord, to receive glory and honor and power; for You created all things, and by Your will they exist and were created"* (v. 11). When the prophet Isaiah described his vision of heaven in chapter 6 of his book, he said that the cherubim angels were crying out in a continual litany of worship, *"Holy, holy, holy is the LORD of hosts; the whole earth is full of His glory"* (Isaiah 6:3).

The favorite activity of all the angels I have seen in my visions of heaven seems to be the worship of God. Angels worship Him constantly. Without ceasing, they sing God's praises. They bow down before Him and worship Him. They obey Him, carrying out His commands and doing His will.

Again, we are not to worship any other person or creature, no matter who tries to persuade us to do so. God alone is worthy to be worshiped and praised! However, we should know that He provides us with divine help in the form of angels. God is with us. He will never leave His children alone. Sending His angels to help us is one of the ways He shows us that He is present with us.

Jesus Christ Is Greater than the Angels

Third, some people believe that Jesus Christ is on the same level as angels, or that He is lower than they are. They may have come to that conclusion after reading this Scripture passage:

But we see Jesus, who was made a little lower than the angels, for the suffering of death crowned with glory and honor, that He, by the grace of God, might taste death for everyone. (Hebrews 2:9)

In this passage, the writer of Hebrews is quoting from Psalm 8:4–5, which talks about God's creating mankind with great worth and dignity:

What is man that You are mindful of him, and the son of man that You visit him? For You have made him a little lower than the angels, and You have crowned him with glory and honor.

Jesus came to earth as a man, but He is both fully human and fully God. He voluntarily set aside the splendor—but not the reality—of His deity. The Scriptures say that He,

being in the form of God, did not consider it robbery to be equal with God, but made Himself of no reputation, taking the form of a bondservant, and coming in the likeness of men. And being found in appearance as a man, He humbled Himself and became obedient to the point of death, even the death of the cross. (Philippians 2:6–8)

Christ became *"a little lower than the angels"* (became a flesh-and-blood man) for our sakes so that He could achieve our salvation. His glory was then restored to Him. The passage in Philippians continues,

> *Therefore God also has highly exalted Him and given Him the name which is above every name, that at the name of Jesus every knee should bow, of those in heaven, and of those on earth, and of those under the earth, and that every tongue should confess that Jesus Christ is Lord, to the glory of God the Father.*
> (Philippians 2:9–11)

We also read in Ephesians,

> *[God] raised [Jesus] from the dead and seated Him at His right hand in the heavenly places, far above all principality and power and might and dominion, and every name that is named, not only in this age but also in that which is to come. And He put all things under His feet, and gave Him to be head over all things to the church, which is His body, the fullness of Him who fills all in all.* (Ephesians 1:20–23)

First Peter 3:21–22 says, *"Jesus Christ...has gone into heaven and is at the right hand of God, angels and authorities and powers having been made subject to Him."* Christ is forever higher and greater than all angels! The Word of God says in Hebrews that Jesus is *"so much better than the angels, as He has by inheritance obtained*

a more excellent name than they" (Hebrews 1:4).
The passage continues,

> *For to which of the angels did He ever*
> *say: "You are My Son, today I have begot-*
> *ten You"? And again: "I will be to Him*
> *a Father, and He shall be to Me a Son"?*
> *But when He again brings the firstborn*
> *into the world, He says: "Let all the*
> *angels of God worship Him." And of the*
> *angels He says: "Who makes His angels*
> *spirits and His ministers a flame of fire."*
> *But to the Son He says: "Your throne,*
> *O God, is forever and ever; a scepter*
> *of righteousness is the scepter of Your*
> *kingdom."...But to which of the angels*
> *has He ever said: "Sit at My right hand,*
> *till I make Your enemies Your footstool"?*
> (vv. 5–8, 13)

Do not let anyone tell you that Jesus is an
angel, that He is on the same level as angels, or
that He is lower than the angels. Jesus Christ is
Lord over all the angels, and all the angels worship Him as God.

Angels Are Distinct from Humans

Fourth, there is a popular idea that human
beings become angels after they die. Yet the reality is that angels are completely distinct from
people. A human is always a human—whether he
or she is on earth or in heaven—and an angel

is always an angel. People who belong to Christ immediately go to be with Him when they die. They will receive a glorious, resurrected body when Jesus returns for the church, but they do not become angels.

The apostle Peter said that angels *"are greater in power and might"* than humans (2 Peter 2:11). Angels were created before mankind, and throughout the Word of God, they are depicted as existing on a level somewhere between God and man.

Billy Graham, in his best-selling book *Angels,* said this about God's special agents:

> Angels belong to a uniquely different dimension of creation that we, limited to the natural order, can scarcely comprehend....[God] has given angels higher knowledge, power and mobility than we....They are God's messengers whose chief business is to carry out His orders in the world. He has given them an ambassadorial charge. He has designated and empowered them as holy deputies.

Angels are a higher form of creation than humans in this sense: Right now, they have higher spiritual knowledge, power, and mobility than we do. In addition, God's holy angels never sin against Him. As long as we are on earth and not yet totally free from *"this body of death"* (Romans

7:24), which is the way the apostle Paul described our tendency to sin, then we are not as morally good as God's holy angels. We still sin and go against the will of God at times. Angels always work directly for God and with God, and they don't sin; therefore, they are "higher" than we are.

When we acknowledge that angels are higher · than we are, we are not putting humanity down. King David recognized the dignity and glory of mankind:

> *You have crowned him with glory and honor. You have made him to have dominion over the works of Your hands; You have put all things under his feet.*
>
> (Psalm 8:5–6)

This passage was so beautiful and important to the early Christians that the New Testament writer quoted it in his letter to the Hebrews (Hebrews 2:7–8), as I talked about in the previous section.

Notice that mankind is *"crowned...with glory and honor."* We were crowned with glory and honor because, first of all, we were created in the image of God. *"God created man in His own image; in the image of God He created him; male and female He created them"* (Genesis 1:27). The Bible doesn't say that angels were created in God's image—only that we were. That makes us precious to Him. Next, mankind was given dominion over all the works of God's hands on earth. God honored humanity by entrusting it with the stewardship and development of the entire world.

Also, we are so important to God that He sent His Son to earth to die for us! He didn't do that for the angels who fell and rebelled against Him. (I will talk more about that shortly.) Hebrews 2:16 says, *"For indeed He does not give aid to angels, but He does give aid to the seed of Abraham."* When mankind fell, God provided a way for us to be forgiven and restored to Him. We have been redeemed through the blood of Christ. This gives us a high and exalted position with God:

> *If God is for us, who can be against us? He who did not spare His own Son, but delivered Him up for us all, how shall He not with Him also freely give us all things?* (Romans 8:31–32)

Because Christ redeemed us, we have the righteousness of Jesus Himself! *"Christ Jesus...became for us wisdom from God; and righteousness and sanctification and redemption"* (1 Corinthians 1:30). Paul wrote of the time after Jesus comes back when Christians will exist in a glorified state:

> *I consider that the sufferings of this present time are not worthy to be compared with the glory which shall be revealed in us....Whom He predestined, these He also called; whom He called,*

*these He also justified; and whom
He justified, these He also glorified.*
(Romans 8:18, 30)

At that time, we will be higher than the angels, and we will even judge them. The Bible says, *"Do you not know that we* [believers] *shall judge angels?"* (1 Corinthians 6:3).

Some of God's Angels Rebelled against Him

⑤ Fifth, as I said earlier, many people think all angels are benevolent. However, we must realize that some of God's angels rebelled against Him, and that is the reason that they will one day be judged. They will be eternally punished at the end of the age.

If all angels were created holy, as God is holy, then what happened? The Bible indicates that, at some point, Satan—who is also referred to as Lucifer or the devil—rebelled against God and was expelled from heaven. Ezekiel 28 is apparently alluding to Satan before he fell when it talks about one who had been *"the anointed cherub who covers* [*"a guardian cherub"* NIV]*"* and who had been *"on the holy mountain of God"* (v. 14). Satan seems to have been one of a special group of angels known as cherubim, but his heart apparently became corrupted by pride:

You were the seal of perfection, full of wisdom and perfect in beauty. You were in Eden, the garden of God; every precious

stone was your covering: the sardius, topaz, and diamond, beryl, onyx, and jasper, sapphire, turquoise, and emerald with gold. The workmanship of your timbrels and pipes was prepared for you on the day you were created. You were the anointed cherub who covers; I established you; you were on the holy mountain of God; you walked back and forth in the midst of fiery stones. You were perfect in your ways from the day you were created, till iniquity was found in you. By the abundance of your trading you became filled with violence within, and you sinned; therefore I cast you as a profane thing out of the mountain of God; and I destroyed you, O covering cherub, from the midst of the fiery stones. Your heart was lifted up because of your beauty; you corrupted your wisdom for the sake of your splendor; I cast you to the ground....I brought fire from your midst; it devoured you, and I turned you to ashes upon the earth in the sight of all who saw you.
(Ezekiel 28:12–18)

Notice in this next passage from Isaiah that pride is again mentioned as being Satan's downfall:

How you are fallen from heaven, O Lucifer, son of the morning! How you are cut down to the ground, you who weakened the nations! For you have said in your heart: "I will ascend into heaven, I will exalt

40

*my throne above the stars of God; I will
also sit on the mount of the congregation
on the farthest sides of the north; I will
ascend above the heights of the clouds, I
will be like the Most High." Yet you shall
be brought down to Sheol, to the lowest
depths of the Pit.* (Isaiah 14:12–15)

Other angels followed Satan in his rebellion,
and they all fell from their sinless position in
heaven. Based on the following passage from Revelation, many people believe that about a third of
the angels of heaven rebelled:

*And another sign appeared in heaven:
behold, a great, fiery red dragon having
seven heads and ten horns, and seven dia-
dems on his heads. His tail drew a third of
the stars of heaven and threw them to the
earth....And war broke out in heaven:* [the
archangel] *Michael and his angels fought
with the dragon; and the dragon and his
angels fought, but they did not prevail, nor
was a place found for them in heaven any
longer. So the great dragon was cast out,
that serpent of old, called the Devil and
Satan, who deceives the whole world; he was
cast to the earth, and his angels were cast
out with him.* (Revelation 12:3–4, 7–9)

The Bible tells us that the fallen angels were
cast into hell to await their judgment at the end of
the age:

God did not spare the angels who sinned, but cast them down to hell and delivered them into chains of darkness, to be reserved for judgment. (2 Peter 2:4)

And the angels who did not keep their proper domain, but left their own abode, [God] *has reserved in everlasting chains under darkness for the judgment of the great day.* (Jude 6)

The Bible also reveals the solemn reality that, even though the angels who sinned were cast into hell, some, at least, continue to operate against God and His people:

For we do not wrestle against flesh and blood, but against principalities, against powers, against the rulers of the darkness of this age, against spiritual hosts of wickedness in the heavenly places.

(Ephesians 6:12)

Satan is the leader of the fallen angels, and Jesus said that the devil *"does not come except to steal, and to kill, and to destroy"* (John 10:10). Satan hates God, and he hates God's people with a passion.

All iniquity on earth stems from Lucifer's sin. In his desire to further hurt God and usurp His authority, Satan tempted God's beloved creation, mankind, so that humanity would also rebel against God and be a fallen, corrupt people. (See Genesis 3.) Humanity did fall, and Lucifer thought he had won a victory. However, the devil did not count on God's sending Jesus to redeem humanity. Now he works to keep lost souls in darkness by blinding them to the truth of the Gospel, which is the message of salvation and freedom from sin through faith in Christ. When Satan rebelled, he exalted himself because he wanted to be worshiped as God. Today, he continues to try to exalt himself.

In fact, I believe that he and his fallen angels are behind much of the current angel craze in our culture. The Bible says that he *"transforms himself into an angel of light"* (2 Corinthians 11:14) in order to deceive people. His purpose is to cause us to worship him and his evil spirits rather than God. He knows that people were created as vessels of worship. Either we are worshiping the true and living God, or we are worshiping the devil and his demon forces. Those who do not know God are serving Satan—consciously or unconsciously.

Satan wants to draw all people to his counterfeit light. Your adversary is lying in wait to deceive you if he can. He wants to confuse you in regard to the truth. Once you are deceived, your mind and heart become open doors for him to attack. That is why it is extremely important in this age, when so many people are becoming interested in spiritual things, that we learn to recognize when the devil is at work and to discern the difference between good and evil angels.

How to Discern the Spirits

How are we to know if what presents itself as an angel is truly from God? The Bible tells us to try or test the spirits to see if they are authentic:

Beloved, do not believe every spirit, but test the spirits, whether they are of God; because many false prophets have gone out into the world. By this you know the Spirit of God: Every spirit that confesses ["acknowledges" NIV] that Jesus Christ has come in the flesh is of God, and every spirit that does not confess ["acknowledge" NIV] that Jesus Christ has come in the flesh is not of God. And this is the spirit of the Antichrist, which you have heard was coming, and is now already in the world. (1 John 4:1–3)

If we continually read and meditate on the Word of God, we can distinguish between the devil's deceiving angels and God's holy angels. You can tell whether or not an angel is from God by what he says about the Lord Jesus and the salvation He provided for humanity when He came to earth as a man and shed His precious, cleansing blood on the cross. If a spiritual being communicates any message that denies the deity, humanity, and salvation of the Lord Jesus, we can unmask him as the enemy. We can expose him through the power of the Holy Spirit. If his message promotes an unscriptural message or practice, if it draws attention to himself rather than Jesus, then that spirit being is a demon attempting to deceive people.

Therefore, if any being, or any person, claiming to be an angel begins to tell you something that is different from God's Word, or that goes against God's Word, you can know that an evil spirit from hell is behind it. Remember that Satan twisted the Scriptures out of context when he tried to tempt Jesus in the wilderness (see Luke 4:1–13), and he is still trying to manipulate the Scriptures to deceive people today. Make it a priority to study and learn the whole Word of God so you can tell when the Scriptures are being misquoted.

While fallen angels are working as hard as they can to do evil under the direction of the devil, righteous angels are diligently serving God and doing good under His direction. God's holy angels continually glorify Him. They acknowledge Jesus Christ and His coming into the world to redeem us from the enemy's bondage. They focus on Jesus and His deliverance. By their activities and actions, they continually emphasize God's work and will.

Our Ultimate Protection against Deception and Evil

Your ultimate protection against the enemy's deception and evil is the Lord Jesus Christ Himself. The final destiny of Satan and his angels is to spend eternity in a burning lake of fire. Jesus said that there is an *"everlasting fire prepared for the devil and his angels"* (Matthew 25:41). It would be Satan's delight to take you and all your friends with him to hell. Let me beg you not to let this happen to you! Believe in the Lord Jesus Christ and accept Him as your Savior today. Then, as you study about angels, pray to God the Father, in Jesus' name, and ask for His direction and protection so that you will not be deceived by the enemy.

Remember that Jesus is *always* more powerful than the devil and his demons because they are only created beings, while Jesus is God. In addition, when we accept Christ's sacrifice on our behalf, we are safe in Him. Romans 8:38–39 says,

> *For I am persuaded that neither death nor life, nor angels nor principalities nor powers, nor things present nor things to come, nor height nor depth, nor any other created thing, shall be able to separate us from the love of God which is in Christ Jesus our Lord.*

When Jesus was about to be arrested and crucified, He said that He could easily call tens of thousands of angels to come to His aid: *"Do you think that I cannot now pray to My Father, and He will provide Me with more than twelve legions of angels?"* (Matthew 26:53). In Roman times, a legion could be made up of between three thousand and twelve thousand soldiers, including cavalry and support staff. Jesus could have destroyed His enemies then and there, but He allowed Himself to be crucified for our sakes. Through His death and resurrection, He restored our relationship with God. He paid a great price to provide us with forgiveness of sin and new life in Him.

Once, when I was diligently praying, I had a vision of the day Christ was crucified. It just broke my heart. I saw the Roman soldiers nailing His hands to the cross using huge nails. I saw His blood dripping and running down. I remember seeing the blood coming not just from His hands but from all over His body. He had been beaten so badly that I wanted to comfort my Lord and do something to help Him.

The men who were doing this terrible deed were cursing and blaspheming Him. All at once, the eyes of the Lord looked up. When He looked straight at the men, they fell backward. After a little while, they continued to prepare Jesus for crucifixion. Then I saw them lift up the Lord on the cross. It was so horrible and sad! I was crying and weeping as I saw this mighty vision.

Then I saw angels by the thousands. They seemed to be invisible to those who were at the crucifixion, but I could see them clearly. The angels placed every drop of blood that Jesus shed in vessels they held in their hands, and then they carried the blood of Jesus to heaven and laid it on the mercy seat. Just as atonement in the Old Testament was made by regularly applying the blood of animals to the mercy seat in the Holy of Holies (Leviticus 16:14–16), so Jesus' blood was applied to the mercy seat in heaven. Yet the Old Testament sacrifices were only a type of the sacrifice of Christ. His blood alone was able to atone for the sins of the whole world once and for all.

The angels were crying as they carried those drops of blood up to the mercy seat. The precious treasure they carried represented a tremendous sacrifice for Jesus. As I watched in awe, I began to cry so hard that I could not see the vision anymore. I was overwhelmed by the awesome price Jesus paid for you and me. When He sacrificed His life, it hurt Him deeply. There was agonizing pain involved. Through this vision, I realized why He gave His life. He knew that He had to carry the weight of the whole world on His shoulders, but He was willing to do it in order to save us from a burning hell. Oh, what He has done for you and me!

I urge you to accept Jesus and His great sacrifice for you. If you do not know Jesus, read the Holy Bible and learn about Him. Understand who He really is. The Bible is the true Word of God, and it says you must be born anew into God's kingdom: *"Jesus answered and said to* [Nicodemus], *'Most assuredly, I say to you, unless one is born again, he cannot see the kingdom of God'"* (John 3:3).

Your sins can be washed away through the atonement Jesus accomplished by shedding His blood on the cross. Even if you think you are the worst person in the world, you can turn to Jesus for complete forgiveness. You can pray, "Jesus, I believe You're the Son of God and my Savior. I believe You died on the cross and rose again so that I can have new life in You. I ask You to wash away my sins through Your cleansing blood and make me clean. Fill me with Your Holy Spirit so that I can now live for You. I commit my life to loving and serving You. Amen."

If you prayed that prayer sincerely from your heart, God will be faithful to forgive you and cleanse you completely. He will give you the gift of the Holy Spirit, who will live within you and enable you to obey and serve Him. You will become a part of God's own family, and His angels will watch over you.

Angels in Action

The activity of God's angels in the lives of His people was not just for Bible times. It continues today. Hebrews 1:14 says, *"Are not all angels ministering spirits sent to serve those who will inherit salvation?"* (NIV). Jesus affirmed the involvement of angels in people's lives when He said, *"Take heed that you do not despise one of these little ones, for I say to you that in heaven their angels always see the face of My Father who is in heaven"* (Matthew 18:10). Psalm 91:9–12 assures us,

> *Because you have made the LORD, who is my refuge, even the Most High, your dwelling place, no evil shall befall you, nor shall any plague come near your dwelling; for He shall give His angels charge over you, to keep you in all your ways. In their hands they shall bear you up, lest you dash your foot against a stone.*

God sends His holy angels to help and protect those who belong to Him—who love and serve Him. Angels have worked for each of you who are the children of God. It is possible that an angel will appear to some of you as you face a special need. All around us, the atmosphere is filled with marvelous, magnificent, heavenly angels, God's messengers and warriors. They are there to assist you, to help you, to lift you up!

I call these special messengers "angels in action." They come in the power of almighty God. They are intermediaries between God and man, and they work for people according to God's will. God sends His angels to strengthen me as I try to encourage people in the Lord through my ministry. I have seen so many beautiful things that God has done through His angels in various church services I have participated in. It is wonderful to see God undoing people's heavy burdens and to see lives changed.

In all my visions of Christ, angels constantly surround Him. I am grateful that God has called me to be His servant and has allowed me to see supernatural visions of angels in action. If you meet someone who doesn't believe in angels, just remember that the same situation existed in Jesus' day: *"Sadducees say that there is no resurrection; and no angel or spirit"* (Acts 23:8). Some people live such cold, mundane lives that they believe God is cold and mundane, as well. They do not realize that *"God is Spirit, and those who worship Him must worship in spirit and truth"* (John 4:24). They also do not know that they are surrounded by a vital and active spiritual realm in which both good and evil angels operate.

The Hour of God's Visitation

We must always keep our eyes on the glory that is being manifested throughout the earth today. This is the hour of God's dispensation; this is the hour of the visitation of the Lord. As the second coming of our Lord Jesus Christ draws closer, I believe that the visible activity of angels will continue to increase here on earth. I have noticed that others have also seen revelations from God and have written books about them. I believe God is preparing international events for the triumph and reign of His Son, Jesus Christ.

I also believe that God is preparing His people for the trouble and turmoil that will come on this earth as Satan attempts a last-ditch but futile effort to prevent the return of our blessed Lord. In this age of uncertainty, upheaval, and loss of control over our daily lives, it is very comforting to know that God has commissioned multitudes of spiritual beings whose principal responsibility is to protect and encourage His people. Jesus is truly the great I AM! Our God is a wonderful God, and He wants us to know how much He loves us, how much He cares for us. Let us ask the Lord to surround us with His holy angels, and let us always persevere in loving and serving Him, for Jesus said,

> *I am coming soon. Hold on to what you have, so that no one will take your crown. Him who overcomes I will make a pillar in the temple of my God. Never again will he leave it. I will write on him the name of my God and the name of the city of my God, the new Jerusalem, which is coming down out of heaven from my God; and I will also write on him my new name.*
>
> (Revelation 3:11–12 NIV)

3

What Are Angels Like?

ngels are often portrayed today as chubby little cupids who look cute and sweet, but this is not the biblical view. In the Bible, those who saw angels were often amazed or overwhelmed at the sight of these magnificent beings.

The Word of God presents a striking picture of the nature, number, and appearance of angels. In the visions and revelations that God has given me, I have seen the manifestation of many of these characteristics.

The Nature of Angels

Angels are a unique creation with specific qualities that reflect who they are and what they were created to do.

Angels Are Spirit Beings

First, angels are spiritual beings, not flesh and blood (although they can take physical form, as I will discuss presently). God *"makes His angels spirits, His ministers a flame of fire"* (Psalm 104:4; see Hebrews 1:7). There are several qualities of angels as spiritual beings that we should be aware of.

Spirits Are Immortal

Spirits are immortal; they do not die, but live eternally. Jesus said,

> *Those who are considered worthy of taking part in that age and in the resurrection from the dead will neither marry nor be given in marriage; and they can no longer die; for they are like the angels.*
> (Luke 20:35–36 NIV)

Spirits Are Not Subject to Physical Limitations

Angels are not subject to physical restrictions as human beings are. As spirits, they are not limited by time or space. Locked doors and solid walls are no barrier to them, and they can appear and disappear. (See, for example, Acts 5:17–23; 12:5–11.)

Spirits Have No Gender

Although we often think of angels in terms of having male or female characteristics, and although they have often appeared to humans in bodily form, spirits have no gender in the sense that they do not marry and have "baby" angels. *"In the resurrection* [people] *neither marry nor are given in marriage, but are like angels of God in heaven"* (Matthew 22:30).

② Angels Are Holy

Second, the Scriptures teach that angels are holy beings.

> *When the Son of Man comes in His glory, and all the holy angels with Him, then He will sit on the throne of His glory.*
> (Matthew 25:31)

> *Whoever is ashamed of Me and My words in this adulterous and sinful generation, of him the Son of Man also will be ashamed when He comes in the glory of His Father with the holy angels.*
> (Mark 8:38)

> *And they said [to Peter], "Cornelius the centurion, a just man, one who fears God and has a good reputation among all the nation of the Jews, was divinely instructed by a holy angel to summon you to his house, and to hear words from you."*
> (Acts 10:22)

> *If anyone worships the beast and his image, and receives his mark on his forehead or on his hand, he himself shall also drink of the wine of the wrath of God, which is poured out full strength into the cup of His indignation. He shall be tormented with fire and brimstone*

55

> *in the presence of the holy angels and*
> *in the presence of the Lamb.*
>
> (Revelation 14:9–10)

Angels must be holy because they serve a holy God. This passage from Isaiah is a compelling picture of how the seraphim reflect the holiness of the Lord:

> *In the year that King Uzziah died, I saw the Lord sitting on a throne, high and lifted up, and the train of His robe filled the temple. Above it stood seraphim; each one had six wings: with two he covered his face, with two he covered his feet, and with two he flew. And one cried to another and said: "Holy, holy, holy is the LORD of hosts; the whole earth is full of His glory!"* (Isaiah 6:1–3)

Angels Are Elect

Third, the Bible describes angels as *"elect."* In 1 Timothy 5:21, Paul wrote, *"I charge you before God and the Lord Jesus Christ and the elect angels that you observe these things without prejudice, doing nothing with partiality."* The word *"elect"* in the Greek means "select" or "chosen." (See *Strong's* #G1588.) Paul's meaning is not entirely clear, but he may have been referring to the holiness and eternal nature of all God's holy angels, as David Jeremiah wrote in *What the Bible Says about Angels:*

God's angels are known as the "elect" angels (1 Timothy 5:21), indicating that God chose to let them live eternally in his heaven. Christians are also called "the elect" (2 Timothy 2:10). The angels themselves will be sent by God to "gather his elect from the four winds" (Matthew 24:31), for we too are chosen for eternal life. We and the angels will share permanent citizenship in God's heavenly kingdom forever.

...C. F. Dickason...says the good angels who did not fall in Satan's rebellion "remain fixed in holiness." They are incapable of sin, just as we will be in eternity. But we will be there in heaven only because the blood of Christ has washed away our sins.

Herbert Lockyer, in *All the Angels of the Bible*, wrote,

The widely held view is that the elect angels are those who retained their purity and obedience when certain of the angels fell. They are the angels who kept *"their position of authority"* and did not *"abandon their own home"* (Jude 6).

Angels Are Intelligent Beings, but Not Omniscient

Next, angels are depicted in the Bible as carrying out God's instructions with intelligence, wisdom, and efficiency. Paul even talked about the language of angels (1 Corinthians 13:1). Yet even though angels have much more knowledge of the spiritual world than we do, they are not all-knowing, as God is. Nothing in Scripture indicates that they are omniscient.

But of that day and hour [of Jesus' second coming] *no one knows, not even the angels of heaven, but My Father only.*
(Matthew 24:36)

To [the Old Testament prophets] *it was revealed that, not to themselves, but to us they were ministering the things which now have been reported to you through those who have preached the gospel to you by the Holy Spirit sent from heaven; things which angels desire to look into.*
(1 Peter 1:12)

Angels know only what God chooses to reveal to them or allows them to know. The Bible teaches that angels learn things by observing God's working in and through His people! Paul wrote about how God uses the church to reveal certain things to His holy angels:

For I think that God has displayed us, the apostles, last, as men condemned to death; for we have been made a spectacle to the world, both to angels and to men.
(1 Corinthians 4:9)

[The purpose is] that through the church the complicated, many-sided wisdom of

God in all its infinite variety and innumerable aspects might now be made known to the angelic rulers and authorities (principalities and powers) in the heavenly sphere. (Ephesians 3:10 AMP)

I believe the angels were amazed when Jesus came to earth as a human being to be the Savior of the world. I think they were filled with wonder to see the extent of Jesus' suffering and the cruelty of His death on the cross. I think they still marvel today when they behold the deliverance that God's Son brings to suffering humanity. When God's people come together for a deliverance service, and His Spirit begins to heal, deliver, and set men and women free, I believe the angels are astounded at all the miracles of God's grace.

Angels Have Superhuman Power but Are Not Omnipotent

The apostle Peter said that *"angels...are greater in power and might"* (2 Peter 2:11) than human beings. Paul also referred to angels as *"mighty,"* saying,

It is a righteous thing with God to repay with tribulation those who trouble you, and to give you who are troubled rest with us when the Lord Jesus is revealed from heaven with His mighty angels.

(2 Thessalonians 1:6–7)

Angels are given great strength and ability by God to carry out His will and commands. However, they are not all-powerful, as He is. They don't have unlimited power or authority, but only what God gives them.

The powerful might of angels is demonstrated many times in the Bible in its depictions of angels working on behalf of God's people and fighting God's battles. Here are several examples:

> *The LORD said to Moses, "...And I will send My Angel before you, and I will drive out the Canaanite and the Amorite and the Hittite and the Perizzite and the Hivite and the Jebusite."*   (Exodus 33:1–2)

> *The LORD sent a plague upon Israel from the morning till the appointed time. From Dan to Beersheeba seventy thousand men of the people died. And when the angel stretched out his hand over Jerusalem to destroy it, the LORD relented from the destruction, and said to the angel who was destroying the people, "It is enough; now restrain your hand."*
> (2 Samuel 24:15–16)

> *And it came to pass on a certain night that the angel of the LORD went out, and killed in the camp of the Assyrians one hundred and eighty-five thousand.*   (2 Kings 19:35)

Daniel said to the king, "...My God sent His angel and shut the lions' mouths, so that they have not hurt me, because I was found innocent before Him."
(Daniel 6:21–22)

He will send His angels with a great sound of a trumpet, and they will gather together His elect from the four winds, from one end of heaven to the other.
(Matthew 24:31)

I saw four angels standing at the four corners of the earth, holding the four winds of the earth, that the wind should not blow on the earth, on the sea, or on any tree. Then I saw another angel ascending from the east, having the seal of the living God. And he cried with a loud voice to the four angels to whom it was granted to harm the earth and the sea.
(Revelation 7:1–2)

So the four angels, who had been prepared for the hour and day and month and year, were released to kill a third of mankind. (Revelation 9:15)

2 The Number of the Angels

Next, how many angels are there? There are various references in the Bible to numbers of angels. In Matthew 26:53, Jesus referred to *"legions of angels"*: *"Do you think that I cannot now pray to My Father, and He will provide Me with more than twelve legions of angels?"* Again, a Roman legion could be made up of between three thousand and twelve thousand soldiers, including cavalry and support staff. Therefore, Jesus was talking about tens of thousands of angels being readily available to come to His aid.

Daniel had a vision in which he saw *"the Ancient of Days"* (Daniel 7:9), or God Himself, on His throne. Daniel said that *"a thousand thousands ministered to Him; ten thousand times ten thousand stood before Him"* (v. 10). That number comes to more than one hundred million! Yet, even then, apparently not all the angels were present because, in Revelation 5:11, John looked at the angels and elders around God's throne and said that *"the number of them was ten thousand times ten thousand, **and** thousands of thousands"* (emphasis added). In other words, there were even *more* than one hundred million. The writer of Hebrews refers to an *"innumerable company of angels"* (Hebrews 12:22). There are too many angels for us to count!

Another reason we know there are multitudes of angels is that they are referred to as "hosts" of the Lord. In fact, numerous times in the Old Testament (285 times in the King James Version), God is referred to as the *"Lord of hosts"* or the *"God of hosts."* In the New Testament, the angel choir that was praising God at Jesus' birth was called *"a multitude of the heavenly host"* (Luke 2:13). The Hebrew and Greek words that are translated *"hosts"* or *"host"* refer to an army, particularly one organized and ready for war. (See *Strong's* #H6635; #H4264; #G4756.) Consider these Scriptures that refer to the Lord of hosts:

> [Hannah] *made a vow and said, "O LORD of hosts, if You will indeed look on the affliction of Your maidservant and remember me, and not forget Your maidservant, but will give your maidservant a male child, then I will give him to the LORD all the days of his life."*
> (1 Samuel 1:11)

> *Then David said to the Philistine, "You come to me with a sword, with a spear, and with a javelin. But I come to you in the name of the LORD of hosts, the God of the armies of Israel, whom you have defied."*   (1 Samuel 17:45)

> *Then Micaiah said, "Therefore hear the word of the LORD: I saw the LORD sitting on His throne, and all the host of heaven standing by, on His right hand and on His left."*   (1 Kings 22:19)

> *O LORD God of hosts, who is mighty like You, O LORD?*   (Psalm 89:8)

> *Bless the LORD, you His angels, who excel in strength, who do His word, heeding the*

voice of His word. Bless the LORD, all you His hosts, you ministers of His, who do His pleasure. (Psalm 103:20–21)

So the LORD of hosts will come down to fight for Mount Zion. (Isaiah 31:4)

O LORD of hosts, God of Israel, the One who dwells between the cherubim, You are God, You alone, of all the kingdoms of the earth. (Isaiah 37:16)

For thus says the LORD of hosts: "Once more (it is a little while) I will shake heaven and earth, the sea and dry land; and I will shake all nations, and they shall come to the Desire of All Nations, and I will fill this temple with glory." (Haggai 2:6–7)

God saves and delivers through His mighty hosts of angels. There is an innumerable host of angelic beings who surround and worship the Lord day and night and who do His bidding.

③ The Appearance of Angels in the Bible

Third, what do God's angels look like? Angels are choice specimens of beauty and grace, reflecting the glory of their Creator. Sometimes, angels are not visible to the human eye as they go about fulfilling God's Word and purposes. At other times, they are visible to us.

Even though angels are spirits, they can take on various physical forms as they carry out God's will. Humans have observed angels (at least) since the fall of mankind when God placed the cherubim in the Garden of Eden to guard the way to the Tree of Life with a flaming sword (Genesis 3:24).

In the Bible, angels did not appear to people as a form of mist or ethereal fog. They sometimes appeared as dazzling, strange, or overpowering entities who could seem frightening, while at other times, they appeared as human beings. These manifestations seemed to be in keeping with the functions and roles they were carrying out. Angels were sometimes seen sitting down, and other times standing up. (See, for example, Judges 6:11; Matthew 28:1–2; John 20:12; Genesis 18:2; Isaiah 6:2; Luke 24:4.) They almost always seemed to inspire awe, however, in those who saw them, as was the case with Samson's parents, who encountered the angel of the Lord:

> *The woman came and told her husband, saying, "A Man of God came to me, and His countenance was like the countenance of the Angel of God, very awesome."...It happened as the flame went up toward heaven from the altar; the Angel of the LORD ascended in the flame of the altar! When Manoah and his wife saw this, they fell on their faces to the ground.*
>
> (Judges 13:6, 20)

Shining or Dazzling Appearance

In the Bible, when the angels appeared in shining or dazzling brightness, they reflected God's own glory. For example, the angel who announced Jesus' birth to the shepherds was accompanied by the glory of God: *"Behold, an angel of the Lord stood before them, and the glory of the Lord shone around them, and they were greatly afraid"* (Luke 2:9). The two angels who appeared at Jesus' empty tomb to announce His resurrection from the dead wore *"shining garments"* (Luke 24:4). When Herod was persecuting the early church and had the apostle Peter imprisoned, *"an angel of the Lord stood by* [Peter], *and a light shone in the prison"* (Acts 12:7); Peter was led to freedom by this angel. In Revelation 18:1, John wrote, *"I saw another angel coming down from heaven, having great authority, and the earth was illuminated with his glory."* God declares and reveals His glory through His angels.

Strange Forms or Features

Sometimes angels in the Bible appeared in strange forms or with unusual features. For example, here is a description of *"four living creatures"* that the prophet Ezekiel saw in a vision. He later identified these beings as cherubim:

> *Then I looked, and behold, a whirlwind was coming out of the north, a great cloud with raging fire engulfing itself;*

and brightness was all around it and radiating out of its midst like the color of amber, out of the midst of the fire. Also from within it came the likeness of four living creatures. And this was their appearance: they had the likeness of a man. Each one had four faces, and each one had four wings. Their legs were straight, and the soles of their feet were like the soles of calves' feet. They sparkled like the color of burnished bronze. The hands of a man were under their wings on their four sides; and each of the four had faces and wings. Their wings touched one another. The creatures did not turn when they went, but each one went straight forward. As for the likeness of their faces, each had the face of a man; each of the four had the face of a lion on the right side, each of the four had the face of an ox on the left side, and each of the four had the face of an eagle. Thus were their faces. Their wings stretched upward; two wings of each one touched one another, and two covered their bodies....As for the likeness of the living creatures, their appearance was like burning coals of fire, like the appearance of torches going back and forth among the living creatures. The fire was bright, and out of the fire went lightning. And the living creatures ran back and forth, in appearance like a flash of lightning.   (Ezekiel 1:4–11, 13–14)

In Ezekiel 40:3, Ezekiel encountered another angel *"whose appearance was like the appearance of bronze,"* and in Isaiah 6:2, Isaiah described the seraphim as having six wings. In 2 Kings 6:17, angels appeared as a defensive army of fiery chariots and horses surrounding Elisha. Daniel saw this vision of an angel:

As I was by the side of the great river, that is, the Tigris, I lifted my eyes and looked, and behold, a certain man clothed in linen, whose waist was girded with gold of Uphaz! His body was like beryl, his face like the appearance of lightning, his eyes like torches of fire, his arms and feet like burnished bronze in color, and the sound of his words like the voice of a multitude.   (Daniel 10:4–6)

John gave this description of an angel he saw in the revelation he received:

I saw still another mighty angel coming down from heaven, clothed with a cloud. And a rainbow was on his head, his face was like the sun, and his feet like pillars of fire. He had a little book open in his hand, and he set his right foot on the sea and his left foot on the land, and cried with a loud voice, as when a lion roars.

(Revelation 10:1–3)

In our everyday lives, we can sometimes lose sight of the power and holiness in which God continually dwells. These depictions of angelic beings remind us that God is glorious and omnipotent, and that He is continually working to carry out His purposes in the world.

Human Appearance

Many times, when angels appeared to people on earth, they looked like human beings. For example, in Genesis 18, angels with the appearance of men accompanied the Lord when He spoke to Abraham about the destruction of Sodom and Gomorrah:

> *The LORD appeared to [Abraham] by the terebinth trees of Mamre, as he was sitting in the tent door in the heat of the day. So he lifted his eyes and looked, and behold, three men were standing by him; and when he saw them, he ran from the tent door to meet them, and bowed himself to the ground, and said, "My Lord, if I have now found favor in Your sight, do not pass on by Your servant."...Then the men rose from there and looked toward Sodom, and Abraham went with them to send them on the way. And the LORD said, "Shall I hide from Abraham what I am doing, since Abraham shall surely become a*

*great and mighty nation, and all the
nations of the earth shall be blessed
in him?"...And the LORD said, "Because
the outcry against Sodom and Gomorrah is great, and because their sin is
very grave, I will go down now and
see whether they have done altogether
according to the outcry against it that has
come to Me; and if not, I will know." Then
the men turned away from there and
went toward Sodom, but Abraham still
stood before the LORD.*
(Genesis 18:1–3, 16–18, 20–22)

The angels who came to rescue Lot and his family
from Sodom—the same angels who visited Abraham in the above passage—at first seemed like
men. (See Genesis 19:1–29.)

In Ezekiel's vision, the angels carrying out
God's judgment also looked like men:

*Then He called out in my hearing with
a loud voice, saying, "Let those who have
charge over the city draw near, each with
a deadly weapon in his hand." And suddenly six men came from the direction of
the upper gate, which faces north, each
with his battle-ax in his hand. One man
among them was clothed with linen and
had a writer's inkhorn at his side. They
went in and stood beside the bronze altar.*
(Ezekiel 9:1–2)

Daniel spoke of his encounter with the angel Gabriel, who had *"the appearance of a man,"* at least at the beginning:

Then it happened, when I, Daniel, had seen the vision and was seeking the meaning, that suddenly there stood before me one having the appearance of a man. And I heard a man's voice between the banks of the Ulai, who called, and said, "Gabriel, make this man understand the vision." So he came near where I stood, and when he came I was afraid and fell on my face.
(Daniel 8:15–17)

When angels appeared in human form, they almost always looked like males, but there is a notable exception to this. The Bible tells of two angels who had the appearance of women. Their rank is not mentioned in the biblical account, but they had wings like the wings of a stork, and the wind was in their wings. They performed their mission in a spectacular way, lifting up a basket of wickedness between heaven and earth. (See Zechariah 5:5–11.)

It seems from the biblical accounts that often even the angels who appeared as men had a certain awe-inspiring quality about them that revealed their angelic nature. However, this is not always the case. We are told to be hospitable to strangers because they may be angels disguised as humans. *"Do not forget to entertain strangers, for by so doing some people have entertained angels without knowing it"* (Hebrews 13:2 NIV).

We may see an angel and not recognize him as one! Perhaps, at these times, the presence of angels is hidden from us to prevent us from slipping into the worship of angels and to keep us focused on our true calling. God wants us to love and serve Him not only in the obvious presence of His holy angels, but also in the presence of human beings, who are precious in His sight. The Bible exhorts us in 1 John 4:20, *"If someone says, 'I love God,' and hates his brother, he is a liar; for he who does not love his brother whom he has seen, how can he love God whom he has not seen?"*

Angels among Us

Friends, the Bible teaches that there are truly angels among us. Sometimes we see them and do not even realize what they are. At other times, we sense their presence and know that they are with us. Then, there are certain times when we think we desperately need them, but they seem to be somewhere else! If we believe the Bible, however, we must understand that angels are always around us. They are helping us, guiding us, and watching over us as they carry out God's will in the earth. Seen or unseen, God's angels always serve Him in love and give Him the glory—and so should we.

I have seen many angels in many different forms. The angels whom God has permitted me to see in the visions and revelations He has given me are amazing creatures to behold. The way they looked always corresponded with the mission they were on. Sometimes I see angels in their spirit forms, and sometimes I see them in "human" form. In their spirit forms, angels appear to me to be transparent, with the outline or shape of a human being. Physical walls are no barrier to them. Light floats around them and through them, and many times this makes it difficult for me to see their facial features distinctly. Often, I see spirit angels like these. Sometimes, however, I see angels with visible wings working with the spirit angels to fulfill the Word of the Lord.

What impresses me about all the angels is that they are continually working for the will and kingdom of God. This is what we must always keep in mind in regard to angels. No matter how magnificent or powerful angels are, we should remember that they are servants of the Most High God, as we are. He alone is worthy to be honored and worshiped.

Part II

The Role of Angels

4

Types and Ranks of Angels

re all angels alike, or are there differences among them? The Bible clearly indicates that the angelic realm includes holy beings called "angels," "archangels," "cherubim," and "seraphim." It also suggests there is an organizational hierarchy of angels and even demons.

In referring to *"legions of angels"* in Matthew 26:53, Jesus made an apparent reference to the organization of angels. As I mentioned earlier, a legion was a unit in the organizational structure of the Roman army. When Paul talked about *"the voice of an archangel"* (1 Thessalonians 4:16), he seemed to be alluding to a hierarchy in which some angels have more authority than others, an archangel being higher in rank than an angel. The Lord's brother Jude mentioned the archangel Michael (Jude 9).

Over the centuries, church tradition developed this hierarchy of angels, which is made up of nine orders or levels of angelic beings: angels, archangels, principalities, powers, virtues, dominions, thrones, cherubim, and seraphim. We can see how this list was formed in part from several of Paul's writings, in which he gave us a glimpse into the organization of angels:

> *For I am persuaded that neither death nor life, nor angels nor principalities nor powers,...nor any other created thing, shall be able to separate us from the love of God which is in Christ Jesus our Lord.*
> (Romans 8:38–39)

> [God] *raised* [Jesus] *from the dead and seated Him at His right hand in the heavenly places, far above all principality and power and might and dominion, and every name that is named, not only in this age but also in that which is to come.*
> (Ephesians 1:20–21)

> *God...created all things through Jesus Christ; to the intent that now the manifold wisdom of God might be made known by the church to the principalities and powers in the heavenly places.*
> (Ephesians 3:9–10)

> *For by Him all things were created that are in heaven and that are on earth, visible and invisible, whether thrones or dominions or principalities or powers. All*

things were created through Him and for Him. (Colossians 1:16)

Believers have held various opinions about the categories and ranking of angels from the time of the early church fathers up to today. But it seems clear from the Bible that there are different types of angels and that angels have various positions in God's kingdom. Just as it is within the body of Christ, it is true among angels that

there are diversities of gifts, but the same Spirit. There are differences of ministries, but the same Lord. And there are diversities of activities, but it is the same God who works all in all.
(1 Corinthians 12:4–6)

Let's look more closely at what the Bible tells us about archangels, seraphim, and cherubim.

Archangels

According to Jewish tradition, there are four archangels: Michael, Gabriel, Raphael, and Uriel. However, there are only two places in the Bible where the word *archangel* is mentioned, and only one place where an archangel is explicitly named:

For the Lord Himself will descend from heaven with a shout, with the voice of an archangel, and with the trumpet of God. And the dead in Christ will rise first. Then we who are alive and remain shall be caught up together with them in the clouds to meet the Lord in the air. And thus we shall always be with the Lord.

(1 Thessalonians 4:16–17)

Yet Michael the archangel, in contending with the devil, when he disputed about the body of Moses, dared not bring against him a reviling accusation, but said, "The Lord rebuke you!" (Jude 9)

Michael, Commander of Angels

Michael is the only angel whom the Scripture specifically calls an archangel. He is also one of only two angels in the entire Bible who are named. The name *Michael* means "Who is like God?" (See *Strong's* #H4317.)

Michael appears in both the Old and New Testaments (Daniel 10:13, 21; 12:1; Jude 9; Revelation 12:7). He is always depicted in the Bible in spiritual conflict with evil and wicked powers. Michael appears to be the supreme commander of the angels who do warfare for God—the "hosts" of heaven.

In Daniel 10:13, Michael is called *"one of the chief princes."* In this passage, Daniel told of an angel's appearance to him in response to his prayers, and what the angel said:

Then [the angel] *said to me, "Do not fear, Daniel, for from the first day that you set your heart to understand, and to humble yourself before your God, your words were heard; and I have come because of your words. But the prince of the kingdom of Persia withstood me twenty-one days; and behold, Michael, one of the chief princes, came to help me, for I had been left alone there with the kings of Persia. Now I have come to make you understand what will happen to your people in the latter days, for the vision refers to many days yet to come."* (Daniel 10:12–14)

Later on in the chapter, we again read that Michael stood with this angel and opposed the spiritual ruler of the kingdom of Persia:

And now I must return to fight with the prince of Persia; and when I have gone forth, indeed the prince of Greece will come. But I will tell you what is noted in the Scripture of Truth. (No one upholds me against these, except Michael your prince.) (vv. 20–21)

In Daniel 12:1, Michael is called *"the great prince"* who stands guard over the people of God at "the time of the end":

At that time Michael shall stand up, the great prince who stands watch over the sons of your people; and there shall be a time of trouble, such as never was since there was a nation, even to that time. And at that time your people shall be

81

delivered, every one who is found written in the book.

In the New Testament, Jude records the sobering fact that when Moses died on Mount Nebo, the devil came and tried to claim his body. But Michael, God's angelic general, withstood the devil and rebuked him in the name of the Lord:

Yet Michael the archangel, in contending with the devil, when he disputed about the body of Moses, dared not bring against him a reviling accusation, but said, "The Lord rebuke you!" (Jude 9)

The archangel Michael also battled Satan in the great conflict recorded in the book of Revelation:

And war broke out in heaven: [the archangel] Michael and his angels fought with the dragon; and the dragon and his angels fought, but they did not prevail, nor was a place found for them in heaven any longer. So the great dragon was cast out, that serpent of old, called the Devil and Satan, who deceives the whole world; he was cast to the earth, and his angels were cast out with him.
(Revelation 12:7–9)

The mighty archangel Michael is always mentioned with respect and admiration by those in the Bible. He should be an inspiration to us to be faithful and obedient to God as we serve His purposes in His kingdom.

Gabriel, Chief Messenger Angel

The only other angel mentioned by name in the Bible is Gabriel. *Gabriel* means "man of God." (See *Strong's* #H1403.) Tradition holds that he is an archangel, although, again, the Bible does not specifically say this. However, he is a very important messenger angel *"who stands in the presence of God"* (Luke 1:19) and plays a prominent role in Scripture.

Gabriel appears in the Bible four different times, and each time his appearance is related to the mission of announcing God's purpose and program concerning Jesus the Messiah and *"the time of the end."* Daniel wrote about his encounter with Gabriel after receiving a second vision from God:

> *Then it happened, when I, Daniel, had seen the vision and was seeking the meaning, that suddenly there stood before me one having the appearance of a man. And I heard a man's voice...who called, and said, "Gabriel, make this man understand the vision." So he came near where I stood, and...he said to me, "Understand, son of man, that the vision refers to the time of the end."* (Daniel 8:15–17)

Daniel also told of another visit from Gabriel after Daniel had humbled himself, confessed his sins and the sins of the nation, and interceded with God for the people of Israel:

> *Now while I was speaking, praying, and confessing my sin and the sin of my people Israel, and presenting my supplication before the LORD my God...yes, while I was speaking in prayer, the man Gabriel, whom I had seen in the vision at the beginning, being caused to fly swiftly, reached me about the time of the evening offering. And he informed me, and talked with me, and said, "O Daniel, I have now come forth to give you skill to understand. At the beginning of your supplications the command went out, and I have come to tell you, for you are greatly beloved; therefore consider the matter, and understand the vision."*
>
> (Daniel 9:20–23)

Gabriel went on to explain to Daniel the events of the *"seventy weeks"* (v. 24) and that they would be a turning point in Israel's history. He interpreted God's purpose and program for the people of Israel and the Messiah. (See verses 24–27.)

In the New Testament, Gabriel announced the birth of John the Baptist to his elderly parents. Zechariah (or Zacharias), a priest, was burning incense in the temple, when

> *an angel of the Lord appeared to him, standing on the right side of the altar of*

incense. And when Zacharias saw him, he was troubled, and fear fell upon him. But the angel said to him, "Do not be afraid, Zacharias, for your prayer is heard; and your wife Elizabeth will bear you a son, and you shall call his name John....He will turn many of the children of Israel to the Lord their God. He will also go before Him in the spirit and power of Elijah...to make ready a people prepared for the Lord." And Zacharias said to the angel, "How shall I know this? For I am an old man, and my wife is well advanced in years." And the angel answered and said to him, "I am Gabriel, who stands in the presence of God, and was sent to speak to you and bring you these glad tidings." (Luke 1:11–13, 16–19)

This same hallowed messenger also announced the birth of Jesus Christ to His mother Mary:

Now in the sixth month the angel Gabriel was sent by God to a city of Galilee named Nazareth, to a virgin betrothed to a man whose name was Joseph, of the house of David. The virgin's name was Mary. And having come in, the angel said to her, "Rejoice, highly favored one, the Lord is with you; blessed are you among women!" But when she saw him, she was

85

troubled at his saying, and considered what manner of greeting this was. Then the angel said to her, "Do not be afraid, Mary, for you have found favor with God. And behold, you will conceive in your womb and bring forth a Son, and shall call His name JESUS. He will be great, and will be called the Son of the Highest; and the Lord God will give Him the throne of His father David. And He will reign over the house of Jacob forever, and of His kingdom there will be no end."

(Luke 1:26–33)

While Matthew, the writer of the first gospel, did not name him by name, it was probably Gabriel who assured Joseph that he should go ahead with his plan to marry Mary:

An angel of the Lord appeared to him in a dream, saying, "Joseph, son of David, do not be afraid to take to you Mary your wife, for that which is conceived in her is of the Holy Spirit." (Matthew 1:20)

It is also likely that it was Gabriel who took messages to Joseph in order to protect the life of Christ until His time:

Now when [the wise men] *had departed, behold, an angel of the Lord appeared to Joseph in a dream, saying, "Arise, take the young Child and His mother, flee to Egypt, and stay there until I bring you word; for Herod will seek the young Child to destroy Him." When he arose, he took the young Child and His mother by night and departed for Egypt, and was there until the death of Herod, that it might be fulfilled which was spoken by the Lord through the prophet, saying, "Out of Egypt I called My Son."...When Herod was dead, behold, an angel of the Lord appeared in a dream to Joseph in Egypt, saying, "Arise, take the young Child and His mother, and go to the land of Israel, for those who sought the young Child's life are dead." Then he arose, took the young Child and His mother, and came into the land of Israel.* (Matthew 2:13–15, 19–21)

Gabriel is often depicted as a celestial trumpet player. This idea probably comes from the Scripture about Jesus' return that says, *"For the Lord Himself will descend from heaven with a shout, with the voice of an archangel, and with the trumpet of God"* (1 Thessalonians 4:16). This verse doesn't say that the archangel will sound the trumpet. However, the archangel does appear to be announcing to the earth that the Messiah has returned.

Gabriel is God's trustworthy messenger angel who stands in His presence and brings important news to His people concerning His plan for the world. This angel's reverence for

God, His Word, and His work should inspire us to love and serve God as He carries out His purposes in our own lives and in the lives of all humanity.

Cherubim and Seraphim

Two special kinds of angels are prominent in the Bible: cherubim and seraphim. Both are connected with the presence of God.

Cherubim

Cherubim or cherubs are not at all like today's popular depictions of them as plump little babies with wings. They are powerful and holy beings. The first time the Bible mentions cherubim is in Genesis 3:24 when Adam and Eve were banished from the Garden of Eden because of their rebellion against God: *"So He drove out the man; and He placed cherubim at the east of the garden of Eden, and a flaming sword which turned every way, to guard the way to the tree of life."*

The origin of the name *cherubim* is unknown, but these angels are closely associated with God. In seven different places in the Bible, we read that our great Lord is the God who *"dwells between the cherubim"* (1 Samuel 4:4; 2 Samuel 6:2; 2 Kings 19:15; 1 Chronicles 13:6; Psalm 80:1; Psalm 99:1; Isaiah 37:16). In 2 Samuel 22:11, David said that when God answered his prayer and came to his rescue, *"He rode upon a cherub, and flew; and He was seen upon the wings of the wind."* (See also Psalm 18:10.)

When God gave Moses the plans for the ark of the covenant, or ark of testimony, in the tabernacle, He instructed Moses to place replicas of two cherubim on each end of the mercy seat, upon which the blood of atonement would be sprinkled:

You shall make a mercy seat of pure gold; two and a half cubits shall be its length and a cubit and a half its width. And you shall make two cherubim of gold; of hammered work you shall make them at the two ends of the mercy seat. Make one cherub at one end, and the other cherub at the other end; you shall make the cherubim at the two ends of it of one piece with the mercy seat. And the cherubim shall stretch out their wings above, covering the mercy seat with their wings, and they shall face one another; the faces of the cherubim shall be toward the mercy seat. You shall put the mercy seat on top of the ark, and in the ark you shall put the Testimony that I will give you. And there I will meet with you, and I will speak with you from above the mercy seat, from between the two cherubim which are on the ark of the Testimony.

(Exodus 25:17–22)

God's presence dwelt between these cherubim in the tabernacle, and from that place, He also spoke to Moses. (See also Numbers 7:89.) The Bible says that curtains and the veil in the tabernacle were decorated with cherubim, as well (Exodus 26:1, 31; 36:8, 35).

When Solomon built the temple in Jerusalem, he decorated it with elaborate and elegant carvings, engravings, and sculptures of cherubim, and he had the temple curtain embroidered with cherubim. (See 1 Kings 6:22–35; 7:29, 36; 2 Chronicles 3:7, 10–14.) In exile in Babylon, Ezekiel saw a vision of the future temple, and it still contained rich carvings of cherubim (Ezekiel 41:18–20, 25).

What are cherubim like? Ezekiel mentioned them in chapter one of his book, but he described them in detail in chapter ten:

And I looked, and there in the firmament that was above the head of the cherubim, there appeared something like sapphire stone, having the appearance of the likeness of a throne. Then He spoke to the man clothed with linen, and said, "Go in among the wheels, under the cherub, fill your hands with coals of fire from among the cherubim, and scatter them over the city." And he went in as I watched. Now the cherubim were standing on the south side of the temple when the man went in, and the cloud filled the inner court. Then the glory of the LORD went up from the cherub, and paused over the threshold of the temple; and the house was filled with the cloud, and the court was full of the brightness of the Lord's glory. And the sound of the wings of the cherubim was heard even in the outer court, like the voice of Almighty God when He speaks. Then it happened, when He commanded the man clothed in linen, saying, "Take fire from among the wheels, from among the cherubim," that he went in and stood beside the wheels. And the cherub stretched out his hand from among the cherubim to the fire that was among the cherubim, and took some of it and put it into the hands of the man clothed with linen, who took it and went out. The cherubim appeared to have the form of a man's hand under their wings. And when I looked, there were four wheels by the cherubim, one wheel by one cherub and another wheel by each other cherub; the wheels appeared to have the color of a beryl stone. As for their appearance, all four looked alike; as it were, a wheel in the middle of a wheel. When they went, they went toward any of their four directions; they did not turn aside when they went, but followed in the direction the head was facing. They did not turn aside when they went. And their whole body, with their back, their hands, their wings, and the wheels that the four had, were full of eyes all around. As for the wheels, they were called in my hearing, "Wheel." Each one had four faces: the first face was the face of a cherub, the second face the face of a man, the third face the face of a lion, and the fourth the face of an eagle. And the cherubim were lifted up. This was the living creature I saw by the River Chebar. When the cherubim went, the wheels went beside them; and when the cherubim lifted their wings to mount up from the earth, the same wheels also did not turn from beside them. When the cherubim stood still, the wheels stood still, and when one was lifted up, the other lifted itself up, for the spirit of the living creature was in them. Then the glory of the LORD departed from the threshold of the temple and stood over the cherubim. And the cherubim lifted their wings and mounted up from the earth in my sight. When they went out, the wheels were beside them; and they stood at the door of the east gate of the Lord's house, and the glory of the God of Israel was above them...and I knew they were cherubim. Each one had four faces and each

one four wings, and the likeness of the hands of a man was under their wings.
(Ezekiel 10:1–21)

Imagine these magnificent beings connected with God's presence, purity, and glory that reflect the majesty of the Lord!

Yet there is a sober note related to cherubim, as well. As I wrote earlier, Lucifer was apparently a cherub before he fell and became Satan. In Ezekiel 28, the prophet was probably referring to the devil when he said he was *"the anointed cherub who covers"* and who was *"on the holy mountain of God"* (v. 14). Because of Lucifer's sin, God said, *"I destroyed you, O covering cherub, from the midst of the fiery stones"* (v. 16). It is almost unimaginable to think of how low Satan fell when he succumbed to pride, rebelled against God, and was cast out of heaven. He went from being an *"anointed cherub"* to *"the dragon, that serpent of old"* (Revelation 20:2) who will be *"cast into the lake of fire and brimstone"* (v. 10). What a terrible fall!

This is a grave reminder to us of the consequences of sin, if even a cherub can have such an end. Yet it is also a reminder of Christ's great sacrifice on our behalf that restores us to the very presence of God as if we had never sinned! As Hebrews 2:16 says, *"For indeed He does not give aid to angels, but He does give aid to the seed of Abraham."*

A Divine Revelation of Angels

Seraphim

Seraphim or seraphs are mentioned directly in only one passage of the Bible. Isaiah vividly described these heavenly creatures:

> *In the year that King Uzziah died, I saw the Lord sitting on a throne, high and lifted up, and the train of His robe filled the temple. Above it stood seraphim; each one had six wings: with two he covered his face, with two he covered his feet, and with two he flew. And one cried to another and said: "Holy, holy, holy is the LORD of hosts; the whole earth is full of His glory!" And the posts of the door were shaken by the voice of him who cried out, and the house was filled with smoke.*
> (Isaiah 6:1–4)

(The angels we read about in Revelation 4:8 who surrounded the throne and cried continuously, *"Holy, holy, holy, Lord God Almighty, who was and is and is to come!"* may be either seraphim or cherubim since they seem to have features of both.)

Seraphim are closer than all the other angels to their Creator and Maker, hovering above the throne of God. These attendants at God's throne seem to dwell in the midst of His holiness. The sight of God on His throne with the seraphim above Him filled Isaiah with a sense of his own sin and unworthiness, and one of the seraphs was sent by God to touch Isaiah's mouth with a purifying live coal from the altar of heaven:

[Isaiah] *said: "Woe is me, for I am undone! Because I am a man of unclean lips, and I dwell in the midst of a people of unclean lips; for my eyes have seen the King, the LORD of hosts." Then one of the seraphim flew to me, having in his hand a live coal which he had taken with the tongs from the altar. And he touched my mouth with it, and said: "Behold, this has touched your lips; your iniquity is taken away, and your sin purged."* (Isaiah 6:5–7)

Of the seraphim's six wings, two pairs cover their faces and feet in the presence of God's brilliant glory, while only one pair is used for flying. In the Hebrew, the word *seraphim* means "burning" or "fiery." (See *Strong's* #H8314.) In the visions and revelations I have received, when I see angels as spirits (rather than in a human form), they always look like fire to me. I believe this is because angels, and especially the seraphim, stand before the One of whom it is written, *"Our God is a consuming fire"* (Hebrews 12:29). In one of his visions, Daniel said, "[God's] *throne was a fiery flame, its wheels a burning fire; a fiery stream issued and came forth from before Him"* (Daniel 7:9–10). Moses reported that *"the sight of the glory of the LORD was like a consuming fire"* (Exodus 24:17). In Psalm 104:4, we read that "[God] *makes His angels spirits, His ministers a flame of fire."*

Seraphim are intelligent beings who celebrate the Holy One of Israel. They are aflame with love for God. Their devotion should inspire deep love for God in us, as well.

Angel of the Lord

I would like to say a brief word here about the term "angel of the Lord" or "Angel of the Lord," which occurs frequently in Scripture. (See, for example, Genesis 16:7–11; Exodus 3:1–6; 2 Samuel 24:16; Zechariah 3:1–7; Acts 12:21–23.) At various times, this term may be referring to one of God's angels, to God Himself, or to the Lord Jesus Christ in what is often called a pre-incarnate appearance. Either way, a reference to such an angel in Scripture clearly deserves our attention and respect.

Sent to Serve

We have seen that there are different types of angels who serve God, and that angels have various positions in His kingdom. All God's angels reflect His greatness, power, and holiness. The amazing thing is that they work on our behalf! Again, Hebrews 1:14 says, *"Are not all angels ministering spirits sent to serve those who will inherit salvation?"* (NIV).

In the next chapter, we will look at some of the specific roles that God's angels fulfill.

5

Ministering Spirits

ccording to the Bible, angels have spheres of authority and certain duties to perform in the heavens and in the universe at large. While the earth is not their native habitat, they do conduct active operations here. Angels travel back and forth between heaven and earth as they do God's will. Jacob saw a vision of a ladder reaching from heaven to earth on which angels ascended and descended (Genesis 28:12). In Part III, I will talk about what I have seen of the activity of angels through the visions and revelations God has given me. These revelations illustrate God's continuing presence and work among His people today.

Yes, my dear friend, angels are in action around us all the time. Things are happening in the spiritual realm that our physical senses cannot detect; these things have to be spiritually discerned.

A story in 2 Kings 6 illustrates this truth. The king of Syria was puzzled and perplexed because the king of Israel always seemed to know his plans ahead of time. When he invaded Israel, God's people were always able to defeat him. The Syrian king thought that there was a spy among his associates, but someone told him that there was a prophet in Israel, Elisha, who knew even *the words that you speak in your bedroom* (v. 12).

> *Therefore* [the king of Syria] *sent horses and chariots and a great army there, and they came by night and surrounded the city. And when the servant of the man of God arose early and went out, there was an army, surrounding the city with horses and chariots. And his servant said to him, "Alas, my master! What shall we do?" So he answered, "Do not fear, for those who are with us are more than those who are with them." And Elisha prayed, and said, "LORD, I pray, open his eyes that he may see." Then the LORD opened the eyes of the young man, and he saw. And behold, the mountain was full of horses and chariots of fire all around Elisha.*
>
> (2 Kings 6:14–17)

With a whole universe of celestial beings, both seen and unseen, surrounding and helping us, we can be both comforted and strengthened.

We should have respect for these agents of God, these created beings we call angels. God puts them in our lives to minister to our needs. Their works and their actions toward God's people should inspire us to persevere in our daily walk with Him.

Worshipers of God

The primary role of all angels is to praise and exalt God and His Son, Jesus Christ. This is because *everything* God has created—angels, people, even nature—was created for the purpose of glorifying Him. The Scriptures tell us—

> *Praise the* LORD*! Praise the* LORD *from the heavens; praise Him in the heights! Praise Him, all His angels; praise Him, all His hosts! Praise Him, sun and moon; praise Him, all you stars of light! Praise Him, you heavens of heavens, and you waters above the heavens! Let them praise the name of the* LORD*, for He commanded and they were created.*   (Psalm 148:1–5)

> *When* [God] *again brings the firstborn into the world, He says: "Let all the angels of God worship Him* [Christ]*."*
> (Hebrews 1:6)

> [John] *heard the voice of many angels around the throne, the living creatures, and the elders; and the number of them was ten thousand times ten thousand,*

*and thousands of thousands, saying with
a loud voice: "Worthy is the Lamb who
was slain to receive power and riches
and wisdom, and strength and honor
and glory and blessing!"*
(Revelation 5:11–12)

*All the angels stood around the throne and
the elders and the four living creatures,
and fell on their faces before the throne
and worshiped God, saying: "Amen!
Blessing and glory and wisdom, thanks-
giving and honor and power and might,
be to our God forever and ever. Amen."*
(Revelation 7:11–12)

When I had a revelation of heaven, the presence of the Lord was so awesome. No matter what
activity the various angels there were engaged
in, they were singing to the Lord and praising
Him. Angels by the seeming millions continually
worshiped Him. There were also, at intervals,
times of silence, times of meditation.

The atmosphere around the throne of God
is always filled with glories, honor, and amens.
The writer of Hebrews said, *"You have come to
Mount Zion, to the heavenly Jerusalem, the city of
the living God. You have come to thousands upon
thousands of angels in joyful assembly"* (Hebrews
12:22 NIV). The four living creatures at God's
throne (perhaps seraphim or cherubim) *"do not
rest day or night"* because they are saying, *"Holy,*

holy, holy, Lord God Almighty, who was and is and is to come!" (Revelation 4:8).

There are endless reasons for the angels to praise and worship God. For example, when God created the world, the angels must have gazed with excitement and fascination on God's mighty acts of creative genius. Job 38 says of that significant occasion that *"the morning stars sang together and all the angels shouted for joy"* (v. 7 NIV). Through their worship of God, the angels inspire us to appreciate God's beauty and majesty and the glory of His creation, as well as all His other wondrous works.

Ministers of God's People

Angels not only worship God, but are also His willing servants. They are God's active agents who do His will day and night as they minister to Him and His people.

Again, the first chapter of Hebrews tells us, *"Are not all angels ministering spirits sent to serve those who will inherit salvation?"* (v. 14 NIV). Angels are servants of the kingdom of God, and they work for all of us who are heirs of God's salvation, as they are directed to by the will and Word of God. If you are a child of God, angels have worked for you, whether you were aware of it or not. Angels will sometimes appear to believers during times of special need. Their protecting presence shows us how much God cares about us. Here are several of the ways in which angels minister to believers.

Bringing Messages from God

First, angels are couriers from God who bring special messages to His people. Let's look at a few biblical examples of this. In Genesis 18:9–14, the angel of God's presence announced to Abraham that his wife, Sarah, an elderly, barren woman, would become pregnant and give birth to a child. The angel of the Lord also reaffirmed to Abraham that through his lineage all the nations of the earth would be blessed. (See Genesis 22:11–18.)

An angel of the Lord appeared to Gideon and told him that he would save Israel from the hand of the Midianites. (See Judges 6:11–14.)

As we saw earlier, the angel Gabriel announced to Zechariah that his wife Elizabeth would give birth to John the Baptist in her old age. (See Luke 1:11–17.) Gabriel also announced to Mary that she would conceive a child through the power of the Holy Spirit who would be the Messiah. (See verses 28–35.) An angel appeared to Mary's fiancé, Joseph, in a dream, assuring him that the baby was conceived of the Holy Spirit and encouraging him to go ahead with his plan to take Mary as his wife. (See Matthew 1:20–21.)

On the night of the blessed Savior's birth, a single angel appeared to the shepherds in nearby fields, bathing them in a glorious light and saying, *"Behold, I bring you good tidings of great joy"* (Luke 2:10). Then, as the angel announced the birth of Jesus,

> *suddenly there was with the angel a multitude of the heavenly host praising God and saying: "Glory to God in the highest, and on earth peace, goodwill toward men!"*
>
> (vv. 13–14)

An angel appeared to Cornelius in a vision and told him to send for Peter so that Peter could preach the Gospel to him. (See Acts 10:1–6.) Philip was instructed by an angel to go to Gaza for the purpose of meeting an Ethiopian eunuch and explaining to him the message of salvation through Christ. (See Acts 8:26–39.)

We can see from these examples that angels bring important news to God's people of His activity in their lives and His plan for the salvation of the world.

Delivering God's Word

⚵ In a related role, angels deliver God's Word to people and also help them to understand it. For instance, angels were involved when God gave the Ten Commandments and the sacred Law on Mt. Sinai:

> *The LORD came from Sinai and dawned over them from Seir; he shone forth from Mount Paran. He came with myriads of*

*holy ones from the south, from his moun-
tain slopes. Surely it is you who love the
people; all the holy ones are in your hand.
At your feet they all bow down, and from
you receive instruction, the law that Moses
gave us.* (Deuteronomy 33:2–4 NIV)

In his address before the Sanhedrin court in Acts
7, Stephen said that Israel had *"received the law
by the direction of angels"* (v. 53). The *New International Version* reads, *"The law...was put into
effect through angels"* (v. 53). Paul echoed this
truth when he wrote:

*What purpose then does the law serve?
It was added because of transgressions,
till the Seed should come...and it was
appointed through angels by the hand of
a mediator.* (Galatians 3:19)

Angels are always true to Scripture in word
and in action. The angel in Daniel 10 stood for the
truth of God's Word. He told Daniel, *"But I will tell
you what is noted in the Scripture of Truth"* (v. 21).
Paul told us, *"But even if...an angel from heaven,
preach any other gospel to you than what we have
preached to you, let him be accursed"* (Galatians
1:8). He knew that if an "angel" begins to tell
you things contrary to God's Word, he is not a
holy angel from God, but a demon spirit who
has disguised himself as one. Remember that
Satan misquoted the Scripture to Jesus during
the Temptation, and he still pretends to be an

104

"angel of light" (2 Corinthians 11:14) in order to deceive people.

When God has shown me His angels in action, He has always pointed me to Scripture that confirms what I just saw. An angel from God will never give you instruction or guidance that deviates from what God has already said in His Word. I will talk more about the role of angels and God's Word in chapter seven.

Bringing God's Guidance

God's angels also direct people's steps and clear the path before them as they do His will. For example, in Genesis 24, Abraham told his servant that an angel would lead him to the young woman who would be the right wife for his son Isaac. *"The LORD God of heaven...will send His angel before you, and you shall take a wife for my son from* [the land I came from]*"* (v. 7).

In Genesis 31, an angel told Jacob that it was time for him to return home after many years of running from God and his brother Esau. Jacob reported, *"Then the Angel of God spoke to me in a dream, saying, 'Jacob.' And I said, 'Here I am.' And He said,...Now arise, get out of this land, and return to the land of your family"* (vv. 11–13).

The angel who spoke to Philip guided him to the right person at the right time who needed ministry:

Now an angel of the Lord spoke to Philip, saying, "Arise and go toward the south along the road which goes down from Jerusalem to Gaza." This is desert. So he arose and went. And behold, a man of Ethiopia, a eunuch of great authority under Candace the queen of the Ethiopians, who had charge of all her treasury, and had come to Jerusalem to worship, was returning. And sitting in his chariot, he was reading Isaiah the prophet. Then the Spirit said to Philip, "Go near and overtake this chariot." So Philip ran to him, and heard him reading the prophet Isaiah, and said, "Do you understand what you are reading?" And he said, "How can I, unless someone guides me?" And he asked Philip to come up and sit with him. (Acts 8:26–31)

An angel gave Philip specific direction on what to do and where to go, but the Holy Spirit was with him and continued to guide him on his mission. It is always God whom we are to look to for guidance. Once again, we are to pray only to God, not to the angels, even though He will sometimes use His angels to guide us.

During services, I have sometimes seen, in the spiritual realm, angels go up and put crosses on certain people's shoulders. God showed me that this means He has called these people for special tasks, that they have been chosen of the Lord. Sometimes the Lord will allow me to call them up to where I am ministering and tell them that God has called them for a purpose. Often, they will say, "Yes, I know that, but I haven't done it yet." I respond, "Well, seek the Lord. He will surely direct your path. He will not forget you."

As we trust in God, He guides all our paths, and one way He does this is through His angels. The Scripture says, *"Trust in the LORD with all your heart, and lean not on your own understanding; in all your ways acknowledge Him, and He shall direct your paths"* (Proverbs 3:5–6).

Comforting and Encouraging God's People

God's angels also comfort and encourage people during difficult times in their lives. For example, in Genesis 16, the Angel of the Lord gently comforted Hagar when she fled from the harsh treatment of Sarah (Sarai):

> *Now the Angel of the LORD found her by a spring of water in the wilderness, by the spring on the way to Shur. And He said, "Hagar, Sarai's maid, where have you come from, and where are you going? She said, "I am fleeing from the presence of my mistress Sarai." The Angel of the LORD said to her, "Return to your mistress, and*

submit yourself under her hand." Then the Angel of the LORD said to her, "I will multiply your descendents exceedingly, so that they shall not be counted for multitude." And the Angel of the LORD said to her: "Behold, you are with child, and you shall bear a son. You shall call his name Ishmael, because the LORD has heard your affliction." (vv. 7–11)

In Genesis 21, *"the angel of God"* (v. 17) comforted Hagar when she and Ishmael were sent away from Abraham and Sarah, and Hagar thought they would die in the desert. (See verses 9–21.)

In Genesis 28, Jacob had a dream in which angels were climbing up and down a ladder from heaven to earth. Through this dream, God used angels to help assure Jacob that he was in the presence of God, that he was at the very gates of heaven. (See verses 11–15.)

On board ship during a violent storm at sea, Paul received encouragement from an angel that God would save his life and the lives of everyone on the boat, and that God would be with him when he was on trial before Caesar in Rome. Paul said,

There stood by me this night an angel of the God to whom I belong and whom I serve, saying, "Do not be afraid, Paul; you must be brought before Caesar; and indeed God has granted you all those who sail with you." (Acts 27:23–24)

Second Corinthians 7:6 says that *"God... comforts the downcast,"* and at times He uses His angels to bring that comfort to His people. On one occasion, I was going through several crises in my life. I was praying as an intercessor and faithfully preaching the Gospel under a heavy anointing, and I read in the Word about the special ministry of angels to God's people.

I was staying in a hotel, and as I went to bed that night, I heard what seemed to be angels singing above my head. These were beautiful voices singing praises to God, and as I lay there, I joined in worship with them. As we praised and worshiped the Lord, the Holy Spirit began to comfort me. He truly is a faithful comforter. There is a verse that says, *"The Lord your God in your midst, the Mighty One, will save; He will rejoice over you with gladness, He will quiet you with His love, He will rejoice over you with singing"* (Zephaniah 3:17).

Suddenly, I realized my room was filled with • angels! God is a comforter, and angels are in action around us doing His bidding all the time. If we will be open and see with spiritual eyes, we will know that we are blessed by God in this way.

Sustaining God's People

Next, God sometimes sends His angels to strengthen and sustain people. Often, this serves to encourage them, as well.

In Genesis 21, the angel of God who appeared to Hagar in the wilderness showed her where to find water for herself and her dying son. (See verse 19.)

When Elijah the prophet was frightened and running for his life from Jezebel, God used an angel to physically sustain him:

> *Jezebel sent a messenger to Elijah, saying, "So let the gods do to me, and more also, if I do not make your life as the life of one of* [the executed prophets of Baal] *by tomorrow about this time." And when he saw that, he arose and ran for his life, and went to Beersheba, which belongs to Judah, and left his servant there. But he himself went a day's journey into the wilderness, and came and sat down under a broom tree. And he prayed that he might die, and said, "It is enough! Now, LORD, take my life, for I am no better than my fathers!" Then as he lay and slept under a broom tree, suddenly an angel touched him, and said to him, "Arise and eat." Then he looked, and there by his head was a cake baked on coals, and a jar of water. So he ate and drank, and lay down again. And the angel of the LORD came back the second time, and touched him, and said, "Arise and eat, because the journey is too great for you." So he arose,*

and ate and drank; and he went in the strength of that food forty days and forty nights as far as Horeb, the mountain of God. (1 Kings 19:2–8)

At Horeb, Elijah encountered God in the *"still small voice"* (v. 12), and the Lord encouraged him and told him what he should do next. (See verses 9–18.)

In the New Testament, we see that God sent angels to strengthen and sustain His Son Jesus while He was on earth. For instance, at the beginning of our Lord's ministry, after He had withstood the devil's temptation in the wilderness, *"the devil left Him, and behold, angels came and ministered to Him"* (Matthew 4:11). Perhaps they also sustained Him because of the presence of wild beasts in that wilderness (Mark 1:13). Near the close of Jesus' ministry, after He had earnestly prayed to the Father in the Garden of Gethsemane that God's will be done, *"an angel appeared to Him from heaven, strengthening Him"* (Luke 22:43).

As it was with Jesus, so it is with us! Remember that God sent manna or *"angels' food"* to sustain the Israelites when they were wandering in the wilderness: *"Men ate angels' food; He sent them food to the full"* (Psalm 78:25). Whether the need is for spiritual or physical nourishment, or both, God always comes through for His children and sustains them in times of need.

Protecting and Delivering God's People

God's angels also protect and deliver those who belong to Him. As we have already seen, the Bible assures us that angels guard the righteous: *"He shall give His angels charge over you, to keep you in all your ways. In their hands they shall bear you up"* (Psalm 91:11–12). *"The angel of the LORD encamps all around those who fear Him, and delivers them"* (Psalm 34:7).

Let's look first at some biblical examples of God's protection. Lot, who is called a *"righteous man"* in 2 Peter 2:8, and his family were protected by angels and kept from perishing with the people of Sodom and Gomorrah:

> *Now the two angels came to Sodom in the evening, and Lot was sitting in the gate of Sodom. When Lot saw them,...he said, "Here now, my lords, please turn in to your servant's house and spend the night, and wash your feet; then you may rise early and go on your way."...Then the men said to Lot, "Have you anyone else here? Son-in-law, your sons, your daughters, and whomever you have in the city; take them out of this place! For we will destroy this place, because the outcry against them has grown great before the face of the LORD, and the LORD has sent us to destroy it."...But to his sons-in-law he seemed to be joking. When the morning dawned, the*

angels urged Lot to hurry, saying, "Arise, take your wife and your two daughters who are here, lest you be consumed in the punishment of the city." And while he lingered, the men took hold of his hand, his wife's hand, and the hands of his two daughters, the LORD being merciful to him, and they brought him out and set him outside the city. So it came to pass, when they had brought them outside, that he said, "Escape for your life! Do not look behind you nor stay anywhere in the plain. Escape to the mountains, lest you be destroyed."...And it came to pass, when God destroyed the cities of the plain, that God remembered Abraham, and sent Lot out of the midst of the overthrow, when He overthrew the cities in which Lot had dwelt.

(Genesis 19:1–2, 12–17, 29)

In Exodus 14:19–20, we read that the Angel of God protected His people from the Egyptian army:

The Angel of God, who went before the camp of Israel, moved and went behind them; and the pillar of cloud went from before them and stood behind them. So it came between the camp of the Egyptians and the camp of Israel. Thus it was a cloud and darkness to the one, and it gave light by night to the other, so that the one did not come near the other all that night.

Daniel was protected by an angel after being falsely accused and thrown into a den of fierce lions with no way of escape. When King Darius went to discover Daniel's fate, Daniel testified to him, *"My God sent His angel and shut the lions' mouths, so that they have not hurt me, because I was found innocent before Him; and also, O king, I have done no wrong before you"* (Daniel 6:22).

Jesus indicated that some angels are assigned to watch over little children. He said, *"Take heed that you do not despise one of these little ones, for I say to you that in heaven their angels always see the face of My Father who is in heaven"* (Matthew 18:10).

Second, the Bible tells us that angels not only give protection, but also provide deliverance for God's people. In Matthew 26:53, Jesus said He could have asked the Father to send twelve legions of angels to deliver Him from the Romans when they came to arrest and crucify Him. However, He allowed them to crucify Him so that He could provide atonement for the sins of the world—for your sins and mine. (See verse 54.)

In Acts 5, when some of the apostles were jailed, an angel opened the prison doors without the guards even realizing it and freed the apostles so they could continue preaching the Gospel to the people:

> *Then the high priest rose up, and all those who were with him (which is the sect of the Sadducees), and they...laid their hands on the apostles and put them in the common prison. But at night an angel of the Lord opened the prison doors and brought them out, and said, "Go, stand in the temple and speak to the people all the words of this life."...But when the officers came and did not find them in the prison, they returned and reported, saying, "Indeed we found the prison shut securely, and the guards standing outside before the doors; but when we opened them, we found no one inside!"*
>
> (Acts 5:17–20, 22–23)

In Acts 12, an angel intervened in Peter's imprisonment and led him in another clandestine jailbreak so that the guards Peter had been chained to didn't even wake up!

> *That night Peter was sleeping, bound with two chains between two soldiers; and the guards before the door were keeping the prison. Now behold, an angel of the Lord stood by him, and a light shone in the prison; and he struck Peter on the side and raised him up, saying, "Arise quickly!" And his chains fell off his*

hands. Then the angel said to him, "Gird yourself and tie on your sandals"; and so he did. And he said to him, "Put on your garment and follow me." So he went out and followed him, and did not know that what was done by the angel was real, but thought he was seeing a vision. When they were past the first and the second guard posts, they came to the iron gate that leads to the city, which opened to them of its own accord; and they went out and went down one street, and immediately the angel departed from him. And when Peter had come to himself, he said, "Now I know for certain that the Lord has sent His angel, and has delivered me from the hand of Herod." (Acts 12:6–11)

Through the visions and revelations God has given me, I have come to understand the subtle difference in the roles of what I call "defensive angels" and "offensive angels." Defensive angels protect us from harm and danger and all kinds of evil devices of Satan. They serve as guardian angels. They protect us even when we don't know they are there. Offensive angels wage active war against strongholds, principalities, demons, forces of darkness, and everything else that opposes the work of God. We'll look at the role of offensive angels in more detail shortly.

Promoting the Gospel

God's angels are also active in promoting the Gospel. They are very interested in the salvation of the lost. In Luke 15, after Jesus told the parable of the lost sheep, He said, *"I say to you that likewise there will be more joy in heaven over one sinner who repents than over ninety-nine just persons who need no repentance"* (v. 7). Jesus repeated this idea after telling the parable of the lost coin: *"Likewise, I say to you, there is joy in the presence of the angels of God over one sinner who repents"* (v. 10).

During the Great Tribulation that will come upon all the earth, a mighty angel will proclaim the blessed Gospel to the nations of the world. John wrote,

> *Then I saw another angel flying in the midst of heaven, having the everlasting gospel to preach to those who dwell on the earth; to every nation, tribe, tongue, and people; saying with a loud voice, "Fear God and give glory to Him, for the hour of His judgment has come; and worship Him who made heaven and earth, the sea and springs of water."*
> (Revelation 14:6–7)

We saw earlier that an angel of God appeared to Cornelius and instructed him how to find Peter, who would tell him the truth about salvation through Jesus. (See Acts 10.) In his conversation with Cornelius, Peter referred to the Scriptures, saying, *"To [Christ] all the prophets witness that, through His name, whoever believes in Him will receive remission of sins"* (v. 43).

This is an important passage of Scripture that again emphasizes for us a key truth about angels. We know from the Bible that a true angel will always promote a message found in God's holy Word. I can't stress this point enough because, again, Satan will try to deceive you and draw you away from the truth of salvation through Christ. Cornelius had a true angelic visitation, and it led to salvation in Jesus for him and all his household.

Let us thank God for the salvation He has provided for us through the Lord Jesus Christ, and for the ministry of His angels in helping to bring the message of the Gospel to those who are lost.

Carrying God's People to Heaven

Another role of angels is that they are spiritual "pallbearers" at the death of God's saints. Believers do not have to transition from life to afterlife alone. Even in our deaths, angels are ministering to us by the will of God. When our pilgrimage on this earth is over, the angels will carry our spirits away to glory, just as they did for Lazarus. Jesus said,

> *There was a certain rich man who was clothed in purple and fine linen and fared*

sumptuously every day. But there was a
certain beggar named Lazarus, full of
sores, who was laid at his gate, desiring
to be fed with the crumbs which fell from
the rich man's table. Moreover the dogs
came and licked his sores. So it was
that the beggar died, and was carried by
the angels to Abraham's bosom.

(Luke 16:19–22)

In a vision of heaven that God gave me, I saw what happens to believers when they reach heaven's gates. If you are a believer, when you die, your soul will leave your body, and angels will convey you to heaven. A book will be opened, and angels will welcome you. Then you will be dressed and prepared by the angels to stand before God.

By the time you are presented to Him, you will be like a perfect young person—even if you were one hundred years old when you died. Who would not want to serve the God who can do this? He will give you back your youth, and He will give you life eternal so that you will never again die.

I also saw that when babies and young children die, their souls are taken to heaven. There they become grown-up, mature, and complete—perfect! God showed me that when babies are killed through abortion, He breathes eternal life into the little ones so that they become complete in Him. I saw angels transporting the souls of aborted babies to heaven, and I saw God making them perfect on heaven's altar. How awesome is our God!

Continually Active

God's angels continually carry out His will, including ministering on behalf of His people. In the revelations God has given me, the angels are always working, but they never seem to toil or sweat. As they work, they show a keen interest in what humans are doing for God and His cause. Let us commit ourselves to loving and serving the Lord with the same zeal and devotion that the angels have. Let us also appreciate the help God sends through His angels to enable us to serve Him as He carries out His purposes in this world.

Defenders of God's Glory and Honor

We have seen that celestial beings worship God and assist His people. A third major role of angels is to help fight God's battles and execute His judgments in the world. I believe that the angels involved in these activities are the "offensive angels" that I mentioned earlier in this chapter. Angels can be fierce warriors who oppose demons and fight individual battles with them, bring divine judgment on people who defy the Lord, and fight physical battles for God's people. There are many biblical examples of angels fighting on God's behalf. For example, we just read how angels were active in the judgment and destruction of the cities of Sodom and Gomorrah. (See Genesis 19.)

Angels were also involved in both the protection and defense of the Israelites when they left Egypt. The psalmist wrote of the Exodus, "[God] *cast on* [the Egyptians] *the fierceness of His anger, wrath, indignation, and trouble, by sending angels of destruction among them"* (Psalm 78:49). In Exodus 33, God said His Angel would defeat Israel's enemies as they conquered the Promised Land:

> *The LORD said to Moses, "...I will send My Angel before you, and I will drive out the Canaanite and the Amorite and the Hittite and the Perizzite and the Hivite and the Jebusite."* (vv. 1–2)

Joshua encountered the help of the commander of God's heavenly army when the Israelites were going up to fight against Jericho:

> *And it came to pass, when Joshua was by Jericho, that he lifted his eyes and looked, and behold, a Man stood opposite him with His sword drawn in His hand. And Joshua went to Him and said to Him, "Are You for us or for our adversaries?" So He said, "No, but as Commander of the army of the LORD I have now come."* (Joshua 5:13–14)

A single angel helping to defend God's people in Jerusalem killed 185,000 soldiers of the mighty Assyrian empire in one night. (See 2 Kings 19:8–35.) The archangel Michael and other angels fought the devil and his demonic spirits. (See Daniel 10:12–13, 20–21; Jude 9.)

Angels were sometimes involved in the punishment of God's people when they disobeyed Him. In 2 Samuel 24, God sent an angel to execute a plague on Israel because David had sinned by trusting in the number of his fighting men instead of the Lord. At least seventy thousand people died before the Lord commanded the angel, *"It is enough; now restrain your hand"* (v. 16). David actually saw this destroying angel. First Chronicles 21 tells us what a terrifying sight that was:

> *Then David lifted his eyes and saw the angel of the* Lord *standing between earth and heaven, having in his hand a drawn sword stretched out over Jerusalem. So David and the elders, clothed in sackcloth, fell on their faces.* (v. 16)

The plague ended when David took responsibility for his sin, built an altar to the Lord, and sacrificed offerings to God, as God commanded him. (See 2 Samuel 24:17–25.)

God's holy angels are zealous for His glory, and they work on His behalf to defeat disobedience and evil in the world. This is a prelude to their role in helping to defeat evil in the end times.

Participants in End-Time Events

④

Fourth, at the end of the age, angels will help bring this world to a culmination as the old heavens and earth pass away and the new heavens and earth come into being.

Angels will, first of all, accompany Jesus when He returns to the earth.

For the Lord Himself will descend from heaven with a shout, with the voice of an archangel, and with the trumpet of God.
(1 Thessalonians 4:16)

For the Son of Man will come in the glory of His Father with His angels, and then He will reward each according to his works. (Matthew 16:27)

Second, angels will harvest the disobedient for the Day of Judgment. Jesus explained the parable of the tares (Matthew 13:24–30) with this sobering application:

He who sows the good seed is the Son of Man. The field is the world, the good seeds are the sons of the kingdom, but the tares are the sons of the wicked one. The enemy who sowed them is the devil, the harvest is the end of the age, and the reapers are the angels. Therefore as the tares are gathered and burned in the fire, so it will be at the end of this age. The Son of Man will send out His angels, and they

123

will gather out of His kingdom all things that offend, and those who practice lawlessness, and will cast them into the furnace of fire. There will be wailing and gnashing of teeth. Then the righteous will shine forth as the sun in the kingdom of their Father. He who has ears to hear, let him hear! (Matthew 13:37–43)

Third, angels will gather together all the righteous for eternal life:

He will send His angels with a great sound of a trumpet, and they will gather together His elect from the four winds, from one end of heaven to the other. (Matthew 24:31)

They will see the Son of Man coming in the clouds with great power and glory. And then He will send His angels, and gather together His elect from the four winds, from the farthest part of earth to the farthest part of heaven. (Mark 13:26–27)

What a glorious day it will be when Jesus returns, and we are gathered by His angels to live with Him forever! Angels are with us while we live on this earth, they will be with us when we die, and they will be with us at the end of the age. Blessed be God, He truly sends His angels as *"ministering spirits sent to serve those who will inherit salvation"* (Hebrews 1:14 NIV)!

God's Revelations

In Parts I and II, we have looked at the nature and role of angels as they are revealed in the Word of God. In Part III, I want to share with you some experiences I have had in seeing the angels of God in action in my own life. God's angels continue to minister to His people today. Again, their activity is not for Bible times alone. It is for you and for me right now as we love the Lord and do His will.

Part III

Revelations of Angels Today

Introduction to Part III

God began to show me the work of angels among His people many years ago when He first called me into ministry. I was in my car ready to go to the veteran's hospital to pray for my brother-in-law. He had had a massive heart attack, and our church was praying for him. The "wind of God" blew, and the pages of my Bible opened up to Isaiah 6:8: *"Whom shall I send, and who will go for Us?"*

I knew God was speaking to me, and I began to weep. In my heart, I understood that God wanted to use me (this was a long time before I saw the revelations of hell and heaven), and I said, "God, I'll go; send me."

At the veteran's hospital, I prayed for my brother-in-law, and I also ended up praying for many of the patients there. God did a creative miracle and gave my brother-in-law a new artery; he lived twenty more years. Because of this miracle, several were saved that day. Truly, the wind of God had directed me.

One day, I began to seek God about the wind, asking, "What is this wind, Father? May I please see it?" God opened my eyes, and I saw what looked like a vapor mixed with glory—a whitish, living wind, a living light. Words were flowing in the wind.

In the old days, Native Americans communicated with each other using smoke signals. The wind of God reminded me of this, as it seemed like a smoke or mist. I could see angels in the wind, and they were carrying scrolls containing the messages God had given them. Some contained orders that God had commanded the angels to carry out. It was awesome to see.

I began to see this manifestation in church services. I'd feel the wind blow. Sometimes, something like a misty rain would come down, and I would know the miraculous was about to happen. I would see angels coming into the sanctuary. Some would come in with scrolls, some with bows, and others with swords. They would stand all around the church and on the platform. As the minister would begin to speak, the angels would stand guard by him. Then I would see things begin to happen in the Spirit. It was almost as if I was looking at a television show or a movie.

Oh, how I love to see the wind of God in action! It is so exciting to see God working in these ways. Truly, His wind is moving all over the land. I believe that God's angels of deliverance are "invading" our cities, our churches, and our homes today with His power.

In the next few chapters, I will share with you some of the things I've seen in the spiritual realm concerning God's angels, along with a few stories of others who have experienced angels in action in recent years. I believe God gave me these revelations to strengthen and comfort His people, to let them know that He is with them. Invariably, people are encouraged when I share these experiences. I know that you, too, will be blessed when you read them. Through His angels, God guards and protects us. Even though we live in an age of uncertainty and upheaval, God is showing us that His Word holds true: *"For He Himself has said, 'I will never leave you nor forsake you.' So we may boldly say, 'The LORD is my helper; I will not fear. What can man do to me?'"* (Hebrews 13:5–6).

I also believe that, through these visions and revelations, God is revealing some important truths for the church, such as the role of God's Word in our lives; the purifying, healing, and judging fire of God; the necessity of intercessory prayer; and the power of God to deliver His people. We must understand these important truths as we draw nearer to end-times events and the second coming of our Lord and Savior Jesus Christ. To Him be all the glory and praise!

6

Angels and Protection

ngels are our spiritual guardians. None of us will ever know, this side of eternity, what miracles God has performed through the angels whom He has sent to protect and care for us. This is the promise God gives us:

Because you have made the LORD, who is my refuge, even the Most High, your dwelling place, no evil shall befall you, nor shall any plague come near your dwelling; for He shall give His angels charge over you, to keep you in all your ways. In their hands they shall bear you up, lest you dash your foot against a stone. You shall tread upon the lion and the cobra, the young lion and the serpent you shall trample underfoot. "Because he has set his love upon Me, therefore I will deliver him; I will set him on high, because he has known My name. He shall call upon

Me, and I will answer him; I will be with him in trouble; I will deliver him and honor him. With long life I will satisfy him, and show him My salvation."
(Psalm 91:9–16)

We are kept by God's power; we are safe and secure in the hands of our mighty Savior! The angels cover us, watch over us, and guard us from countless evils. Angels also protect our children; mine have been protected many times through the power of almighty God. What amazing things angels do to protect God's people! They keep us from more foes than we could ever imagine. As Psalm 91 encourages us, let us be sure to set our love upon God and know His name, for He honors those who honor Him.

Protection from Injury

I have seen God's angels protect my family from injury. One time, my son traveled to work on his motorcycle. At about two o'clock that afternoon, I wasn't even thinking of him as I prayed in my house. Suddenly, the Spirit prompted me to intercede in a special way, and I began to really pray in earnest in the Holy Spirit. I didn't understand all of what I was praying, only a part of it.

At about five o'clock, my son pulled up in the yard on his motorcycle and said, "Mom, have you been praying for me?"

I said, "I have been praying for somebody. I didn't know specifically that it was for you; God just prompted me to intercede."

"Well, Mom, I just want you to know this. About an hour and a half ago, I was driving down Tropical Trail at fifty to sixty miles per hour on my motorcycle. As I came around a corner, a large semi truck turned across the street in front of me. Mother, I'm telling you that God was with me. As the semi turned, I realized I had to do something or I would crash into it. So I turned my bike on its side and *went underneath the semi!* I then rode off into a field unharmed!"

"Oh!" I gasped.

He said, "The only thing that happened was that my mirror came off my bike, and I hurt my leg a little bit. But it's okay."

I began to cry. I hugged him and thanked God for him. I have beautiful sons, and I have found that, many times, our children's safety depends on us. If we will press into God in prayer, He is right there for us. We need to pray for our children that God will manifest Himself to them. I rejoice in the protection my family has received from His angels in action. I am thankful that the angels shielded my son that day so many years ago. To God be the glory, and praises be to His righteous and holy name.

Protection from Persecution

Angels often come to us in unassuming ways and in unexpected works. At times, we don't even realize that a heavenly visitor is protecting us. Dr. Billy Graham, in his book *Angels,* relates a story first told by his wife's father, Dr. L. Nelson Bell, a missionary doctor, of a Chinese bookstore operator and his encounter with an angel:

The incident occurred in 1942, after the Japanese had won control of certain areas of China. One morning around nine o'clock, a Japanese truck stopped outside the bookroom. It was carrying five marines and was half-filled with books. The Christian Chinese shop assistant, who was alone at the time, realized with dismay that they had come to seize the stock. By nature timid, he felt this was more than he could endure.

Jumping from the truck, the marines made for the shop door; but before they could enter, a neatly dressed Chinese gentleman entered the shop ahead of them. Though the shop assistant knew practically all the Chinese customers who traded there, this man was a complete stranger. For some unknown reason the soldiers seemed unable to follow him, and loitered about, looking in at the four large windows, but not entering. For two hours they stood around, until after eleven, but never set foot inside the door. The stranger asked what the men wanted, and the Chinese shop assistant explained that the Japanese were seizing stocks from many of the book shops in the city, and now this store's turn had come. The two prayed together, the stranger encouraging him, and so the two hours passed. At last the soldiers climbed into their truck and drove away. The stranger also left, without making a single purchase or even inquiring about any items in the shop.

Later that day the shop owner, Mr. Christopher Willis (whose Chinese name was Lee), returned. The shop assistant said to him, "Mr. Lee, do you believe in angels?"

"I do," said Mr. Willis.

"So do I, Mr. Lee." Could the stranger have been one of God's protecting angels? Dr. Bell always thought so.

Protection in Ministry

Many times, God protects His people as they minister the Gospel. In an earlier chapter, we read how the apostles were delivered from prison so they could continue preaching God's Word.

I know the angels protect me as I am ministering. One time, a little boy came up to me after a service and said, "Mary, I saw an angel standing by you—a huge angel. He was standing behind you, on the back of the platform. He was so big that he was taller than the ceiling."

I looked at the ceiling, and it had to be thirty feet high.

"Although he was tall, I could see his head," the little boy continued, "which looked as if it was going through the ceiling. His arms were crossed, and he had a very determined look on his face. The angel had a sword of fire by his side, and if the devil or any of the spirits tried to come near you, he would pull out the sword and would *cremate* them."

Cremate is the word the little boy used to describe what he saw. It reminds me of the Scripture, *"You shall trample the wicked, for they shall be ashes under the soles of your feet"* (Malachi 4:3).

Protection from Our Enemies

Sometimes, God sends His angels to protect us when we feel most vulnerable. Corrie ten Boom, a spiritual hero of the twentieth century, spent many years after World War II traveling around the world telling about her sufferings and witness for Christ in a Nazi concentration camp. God often intervened in difficult situations by sending angels in answer to her prayers. One of those times was when she was being processed into the camp at Ravensbruck, as she described in her book *Tramp for the Lord*:

It was the middle of the night when Betsie and I reached the processing barracks. And there, under the harsh ceiling lights, we saw a dismaying sight. As each woman reached the head of the line she had to strip off every scrap of clothes, throw them all onto a pile guarded by soldiers, and walk naked past the scrutiny of a dozen guards into the shower room. Coming out of the shower room she wore only a thin regulation prison dress and a pair of shoes.

Our Bible! How could we take it past so many watchful eyes?

"Oh, Betsie!" I began—and then stopped at the sight of her pain-whitened face. As a guard strode by, I begged him in German to show us the toilets. He jerked his head in the direction of the shower room. "Use the drain holes!" he snapped.

Timidly Betsie and I stepped out of line and walked forward to the huge room with its row on row of overhead spigots. It was empty, waiting for the next batch of fifty naked and shivering women.

A few minutes later we would return here stripped of everything we possessed. And then we saw them, stacked in a corner, a pile of old wooden benches crawling with cockroaches, but to us the furniture of heaven itself.

In an instant I had slipped the little bag over my head and, along with my woolen underwear, had stuffed it behind the benches....

Of course when I put on the flimsy prison dress, the Bible bulged beneath it. But that was His business, not mine. At the exit, guards were feeling every prisoner, front, back, and sides. I prayed, "Oh, Lord, send your angels to surround us." But then I remembered that angels are spirits and you can see through them. What I needed was an angel to shield me so the guards could not see me. "Lord," I prayed again, "make your angels untransparent." How unorthodox you can pray when you are in great need! But God did not mind. He did it.

The woman ahead of me was searched. Behind me, Betsie was searched. They did not touch or even look at me. It was as though I was blocked out of their sight.

A Protective Covering of Blood

There is something we must realize about calling on God for protection: Our salvation in Christ includes the protective covering of His precious blood. I have learned that when we are praying for people, and God impresses upon us to cover people with the blood, we should say, "I cover you with the blood of Jesus, the covenant of God!" This means that Jesus Christ is the Son of God who was sent from heaven. He knew His purpose and His destiny. He was sent to give His life on a cruel cross for you and me, so that we could have eternal life. He died so that our sins could be washed away. God has shown me the importance of the Cross and the blood covenant with its accompanying covering.

When we pray or command a covering of His blood, we are affirming that we believe Jesus provided a covering for us and our families through the Atonement. The angels go to us immediately and seal and protect us. Through the blood covenant, we build a hedge of protection around our families and ourselves!

Another thing was revealed to me. When we dedicate someone or something to the Father, the Son, and the Holy Spirit—when we really mean this and anoint the person or thing with oil—we are saying, "This is God's territory." In the Spirit, I've seen that angels fly down from heaven and erect crosses when we do this. When spiritual enemies try to come, they have to back up when they confront the crosses because that territory has been dedicated to God.

Look with Eyes of Faith

Rejoice, saints! God sends His angels to protect you when the devil would try to do you harm. *"He has delivered us from the power of darkness and conveyed us into the kingdom of the Son of His love"* (Colossians 1:13). Look with eyes of faith and see the spiritual bodyguards God has placed around you. Believe in God and call on His name!

7

Angels and God's Word

hen a believer is true to the Word and to the
Lord's witness, God sends His angels, in
answer to prayer, to help and rescue him.
Remember that Psalm 91:14–15 says, *"Because he
has set his love upon Me, therefore I will deliver
him; I will set him on high, because he has known
My name. He shall call upon Me, and I will answer
him."*

The following visions and revelations illustrate how angels affirm God's Word and how
God helps us when we believe and obey His commands. In a previous chapter, we saw how the
angels took part in the giving of the Ten Commandments and the sacred Law on Mt. Sinai.
The Bible says that Israel *"received the law by
the direction of angels"* (Acts 7:53) and that *"the
law...was appointed through angels"* (Galatians
3:19). In the Scriptures, the angels have a special
role in honoring God's Word and conveying it to

His people. Angels are involved in helping us to understand the Scriptures, as well.

God's Word Is True

On one occasion, I saw a vision of a large, white table way off in the distance. It was about six feet by twelve feet in dimension, and it was suspended in the air. I could see people standing all around the table, looking at it. The table itself was higher than the people were tall, so that some of those looking at it were standing on their tiptoes. Others were sitting in high chairs, gazing at the table; but they were all asking questions of one another.

As I drew closer to them, I could see angels standing behind them. Drawing closer still, I could suddenly see the vision clearly. I could see that the big table was an open Bible. The huge Bible represented the Word of the living God. The Lord explained to me that the various people looking at it had different views of what the Bible meant. One person would say one thing, and someone else would say another.

They were all curious about the Bible, and I was glad to see that. Many questions arose among them about certain things in the Word, and they were looking for answers. The angels standing behind the people seemed to be guiding them in their search for the truth. But the vision represented the fact that what God said, He means. We cannot change or alter His Word.

Pulpits of Fire

Often, in a church service, I will see angels writing in large books. Sometimes the angels are standing by individuals and sometimes they are not. At times, they are standing beside the minister who is prophesying, and they're recording what he says. I will see an image of a Bible superimposed on the minister's chest. I believe this means that the Word of God, the open Bible, is in his heart.

In the places where I have preached during the past few years, I have seen, in the spiritual realm, pulpits that had God's fire upon them and pulpits that looked dirty and unclean. I have observed that behind the pulpits that were full of fire were holy men and women of God who revered and honored Him and who wanted things *"done decently and in order"* (1 Corinthians 14:40). These men and women had a holy fear of doing anything against God. They were afraid to harm or hurt Him or His cause deliberately in any way. These men and women truly exhibited the love of Christ. They were so wonderful to the servants of God who came in to minister with them. They would take good care of them and encourage them.

It also seemed that, in every place where I saw God's fire on the pulpit, I would see angels touching the pulpit at various times and worshiping God. Often, I would see them holding one hand to heaven (sometimes both of them) as they magnified the Lord.

I kept returning to churches like this, and one day, during a service, the glory of God rolled in with a mighty revelation. I saw angels come into the church with a large cross that looked about fifteen feet high. They went to the pulpit, which appeared to be on fire. The angels seemed to dig around in the floor, and then they anchored the cross in front of the pulpit. The cross was solid, but fire shot out of both ends and the top of it. I saw this revelation several times, and each time, there would be a great deliverance. Many people would come to the altar, get saved, and be delivered in a marvelous way. It was an awesome sight.

I wondered about what I had seen, so I began to ask the Lord, "God, what is all of this? What does this mean in the holy Word of God?" He said to me,

> These pulpits that you see with the fire upon them represent pulpits where My true Word is being preached. These holy, anointed ministers are purifying the flock with the Word of God and the cross that you see. Therefore, I have established the cross there, and the Spirit is with them for the purposes of deliverance and for the Word of God to be fulfilled. This is a sign that things will happen

that they have been asking Me to do, and it means they are preaching the pure, holy Word of God through the eternal and mighty power of the Cross.

All over the land, I would see the same revelation. Again, as I observed the angels in action, it was almost like watching a movie screen. In many places, I would see angels come in like a cleanup crew and begin to sweep evil powers out of the churches. They would break the bonds of people and liberate them. At one service, some people took pictures, and when they were developed, you could see fire around the people we were praying for. It was a brilliant red in color, and I was excited because it showed the revelation knowledge of the blood of Jesus Christ. It was awesome for me to see these angels working in the spirit realm for God. While it excited me to see these things happen, they did not occur in all the churches or all the meetings.

The Altar of the Heart

One time, I was on a ministry trip with a friend who is a preacher and has the gift of prophecy. We stopped for the night at a motel in a small town. She quickly fell asleep, and I began to seek God. The glory of the Lord came in the room like a fire, and I sat up in bed. Suddenly, I saw an old-time altar, a stone altar, such as people built in

Bible days. It was high and obviously designed for offering sacrifices.

The altar was suspended about two feet in the air, and it was on fire. Flames were visible all around the approximately four-foot-wide structure, but it wasn't being burned up. I got out of bed, and as I looked at the altar, I saw a vision of the presence of God. Books were open in front of Him as He spoke to me:

> My child, I've called you and chosen you to have dreams, visions, and revelations in order to show you mysteries. I have shown you heaven. I have shown you what happens to people when they go to hell. All over the land, I have shown you these things; yet all over the land, many places are not preaching the truth. They do not tell the truth to the people. They have polluted altars. I have appointed you to go through the land and rebuild the altars. "Stand in the ways and ask for the old paths, where the good way is, and walk in it." (See Jeremiah 6:16.) You are to rebuild the old ways and reopen the old paths. You are to rebuild the altars of God.

As God spoke to me, the appearance of His presence kept flaming up, and I thought, *The altars of God can never be burned up. They can never be destroyed. The wicked altars will fall.*

They are tempered with inferior mortar and bad bricks, and they are going to crumble.

God began dealing with me about the altars of the heart. He said that when people kneel in church and seek God for themselves, each person is all alone with God and is saying, "God, here I am at the altar; this is me, Lord. I have these problems. I am a sinner. I've done this; I've done that." Then God said to me,

As they pour out their hearts to Me at the altar, they are making themselves an altar to Me. This is the altar of the heart. I want to clean out the altars in the hearts—the idolatry, the witchcraft, the sorcery, whatever evil they are doing. I want it out of them. I want those who seek Me to tell Me the truth because truth and righteousness can meet together. I want them to tell Me the truth so I can set them free through My Son, Jesus Christ.

As they begin to confess these things to Me and make a new commitment to Me, I will wash away the debris by My fire, by My Spirit, by My Word. They will feel light and happy because deliverance will have come in the name of My Son, Jesus Christ. When they arise from that physical altar, they will have built a new altar to Me.

When you go over the world and talk about hell, the judgment of God, the fierceness of God, and what happens to people when they go to hell, this helps them to understand that they must be sincere with Me and with their souls. This helps them to understand who I am and what I mean. I'm a holy and righteous God, and they shall have no other gods before Me.

Child, many people are never taught these truths. They have ears to hear but do not hear, and eyes to see but do not see. But to you revelations, mysteries, knowledge, and truth shall be revealed. The Scriptures will back up the revelations I will give you, and these Scriptures shall be very important to the world. The Word of God is in action, and this book on angels in action shall bless many to give them strength and encouragement.

In the Bible, God wanted people to repent and tear down the unclean altars in their lives. I began to understand that this is exactly what the visions are all about. God is calling His people to tell the truth and tear down the altars of idolatry.

This is God's divine purpose for all ministries. All ministers, in particular, are called to do this—to obey God and His Word, to go forth and speak His judgments in right ways, and to be faithful in telling people to repent and get right with Him. May this book accomplish what God intends!

The Power of the Word

Another phenomenon I saw in my travels really amazed me. I would see a true prophet of God speak, and he would be covered with a transparent flame of fire. I would see an image of the Bible opened up in his heart, with the Word written there. An angel would be by his right shoulder, and this angel would pour fire on the prophet's head. The fire would go down to the Word in his heart, and he would begin to prophesy. As the Word came out of his mouth, it would turn into a sword. (See Ephesians 6:17; Hebrews 4:12.) Inside the sword was the written Word of God.

When the prophet of God spoke, the Word would shoot out into the congregation, and the congregation would become alive and animated. The Lord showed me that when He speaks, He speaks things into existence, and things begin to happen.

For example, I saw a prophet prophesying, saying,

> I am the Lord thy God who healeth thee; I, the Lord, am here to do great works with thee. I am here for thee, to set you free, to undo your burdens. I am here to rebuke thee, to love thee, to lift thee up.

151

Everything the prophet said would move out over the congregation and fall on the people. Truth and righteousness had met together, and things began to happen. Angels appeared all around and began ministering to the people, some of whom would fall down under the power of God.

On some of the people, I saw black spots. The angels took the power to these afflicted people. They would lay the fire on the black spots, and it would burn out the sicknesses. People were healed, and people were "slain in the Spirit." Through these experiences, I began to understand revelation knowledge of God's Word in 1 Corinthians about the gifts of the Spirit. (See chapter 12.)

It was wonderful to see what God did—and *is* doing. It is awesome when the joy bubbles up in us and the laughter begins to come as we see the acts of almighty God and those of His angels at work. The Word and the Spirit work together with the vessels God chooses to minister through.

In a service in Ohio, some people took pictures of me while I was preaching about the living Word of God. I reminded the people that we must believe God's Word, repent of our sins, and turn back to God—that we must believe the blood of Jesus will cleanse us if we've sinned.

When one of the photos was developed, you could see the outline of a large open book in the picture. It was huge—it looked as if it were about ten feet high. The book was pure white, and it was lifted up over the heads of the people in the congregation. I knew that it represented the living Word of God.

I also have a photo of a little girl from Big Piney, Wyoming, who was about twelve years old and who wanted the baptism in the Holy Spirit. We actually captured on film a white cloud rolling in over this little child, coming near her as she was baptized in the Holy Spirit.

When the cloud came over her, she was lying on the floor, praying. Her little friend was sitting beside her and praying with her. She seemed to go to sleep in the Lord for quite a while. When she got up, she came to me and said, "Mrs. Baxter, can I preach?"

I saw the glory of the Lord upon her, and I asked, "What is it, honey?"

She said, "Well, when I was down there, Jesus came and talked to me. He took me and showed me hell. He showed me how awful hell was, and how we have to believe. We've got to believe it because it's real. It's a true story."

She began to weep, and all the other children began to cry with her. The Holy Spirit fell on them, and they began to groan and travail in the Spirit, praying for people to be saved and to be born again. I could see angels above and around the children.

As we witnessed the works of God, I knew that we were to give God all the glory and praise for them, and to understand that His Word is still marching on, no matter what!

The Word and Salvation

One time, I had been praying to the Lord concerning my family members who were unsaved. Perhaps you, too, have family members who are not ready to meet the Lord, and you are concerned about their souls. While I was seeking God that day, He gave me a special revelation.

I could see sacred books. The angels would open up a book and turn a page, and I could see the written Word of God on it. Flames came out of the book, along with what looked like a mist. It seemed as if glory and power were intermingling with white and red flickers of fire. I knew this meant that I was seeing the living Word of God.

I believe the purpose of this revelation was to convey that what God has said in His Word, He *will* accomplish. He has promised us, *"Great shall be the peace of your children"* (Isaiah 54:13). He has said that He will *"love you and bless you and multiply you; He will also bless the fruit of your womb"* (Deuteronomy 7:13). That is exactly what my blessed Lord does! Keep believing that God will save your loved ones, and give Him the glory for it.

The Word's Power over Satan

I have seen visions in which demon powers and evil spirits were fighting with angels. The angels would always win because they would quote the Word of God. The Word is *"the sword of the Spirit"* (Ephesians 6:17) and defeats the enemy. Remember that Jesus quoted the truth of the Scripture to Satan during His wilderness temptation. The devil had no more ammunition and had to leave Him.

The following is an experience I had in which God taught me the power of the Word over Satan. One time, I went to Miami with a few others to a Christian convention. There was great oppression in the area; evil powers could be felt in certain parts of the city, and I was grieved. We could feel the oppression mostly when we were eating dinner or at nighttime. I wondered, *God, why do we feel such evil when the power of God is so great here in the convention?*

There was a woman at the convention who had been scheduled to share a room with me, but for some reason did not. One evening, she came up to me and said, "I'm a witch. I came to your Christian convention acting like a Christian so I could find out what all you Christians are doing. I want to take it back into the coven so we can work witchcraft against this atmosphere and stop what you are doing."

I said, "Oh, really." Then I began to quote God's Word to her. I said, "Listen, lady, there's nothing you can do to harm me or to harm this meeting. *'God is for us, who can be against us?'* (Romans 8:31)."

She became angry at me and stormed away. I thanked God that she was prevented from staying in my room. I was in a room alone so I could have a quiet place and the time to better understand the oppression and what we were feeling.

On the way back home, we had to travel by car, and I got into the back seat. I thought I would rest for a while, so I began to pray to God about this situation. As I looked up into heaven, first the glory came, and then I saw a mighty vision of the Lord. He was in the middle of a brilliant white light, with glory and power all around Him. The white light symbolized purity; God is so pure and holy.

I saw Him step out of the heavens and into the sky, and I saw His right hand go down. From each of His fingertips I saw power like I had never seen before; this power turned into swirls of energy and fire. Then he put down His left hand. Again, from His fingers and even His thumb, fire shot out. It also came from the palm of His hand and went through the universe like a river of fire.

He said to me, "I have destroyed their works through this fire and My Word. At times, I will step out and fight for My children Myself." I began to shout aloud and praise the Lord. He said to me,

> Child, when you pray, curse the works of darkness. There will be witchery, sorcery, and other evil things planted against people and their works. I want you to pray for their souls to be saved. Ask Me to have mercy on them and save their souls. You never curse the people, just the works of darkness and their activities. Stand on My Word, and My power and might will fulfill it. Believe Me, and I will send forth this fire, and I will cause the wicked to be ashes under your feet. (See Malachi 4:3.)

I praised Him more! I thanked Him and rejoiced. I could feel a lifting and the presence of God that was so joyful. Then I saw an army of angels coming down from heaven with flags and banners and crosses. They were putting up crosses and claiming the land back for the Lord. I thought, *Wow, Lord, how beautiful to behold!*

The Word Is Always Accomplishing Something

On another occasion, I had a vision in which I saw the angels holding up the Word of God—a large, complete, open Bible—in the universe. Flames were coming out of it. It was so large and beautiful! "The Word of God" was written in big letters inside the flames on the pages. One of the pages turned into a picture, and what looked like power radiated from it. Then the pages turned into a large horn (it looked like a trumpet) that stretched out a long way. I could see power, glory, and honor coming from the end of the horn. I knew this meant that it was the living Word of God. I thought, *Oh, God, You are so wonderful! You are the Word.*

I believe that, through this vision, God was telling me to *"blow the trumpet in Zion"* (Joel 2:15), to *"cry aloud, spare not; lift up your voice like a trumpet; tell My people their transgression, and the house of Jacob their sins"* (Isaiah 58:1), so that they will return to Him.

I have seen this large book with its pages open many times in the Spirit. Out of this book would come the Word of God in action. The Word was always accomplishing something for the Lord. Truly, the Word of our God is powerful:

> *For I am the LORD. I speak, and the word which I speak will come to pass.*
> (Ezekiel 12:25)

> *For the word of God is living and powerful, and sharper than any two-edged sword, piercing even to the division of soul and spirit, and of joints and marrow, and is a discerner of the thoughts and intents of the heart.* (Hebrews 4:12)

We often don't realize the power of God's Word. God wants to accomplish many things *"by the word of His power"* (Hebrews 1:3). We should reverence His Word, as His angels do, believing and obeying it, so that He will bring it to pass in our lives and the lives of those we minister to.

8

Angels and God's Fire

Recently, I have been seeking God about His fire—the fire of the Holy Spirit. I have learned that it is both a fire of revival, purification, and healing for His people—and a fire of judgment for those who reject Him. John the Baptist said,

> I indeed baptize you with water unto repentance, but He who is coming after me is mightier than I, whose sandals I am not worthy to carry. He will baptize you with the Holy Spirit and fire. His winnowing fan is in His hand, and He will thoroughly clean out His threshing floor, and gather His wheat into the barn; but He will burn up the chaff with unquenchable fire. (Matthew 3:11–12)

A Fire of Revival, Purification, and Healing

The prophet Joel prophesied of the baptism with the Holy Spirit:

Then you shall know that I am in the midst of Israel: I am the LORD your God and there is no other. My people shall never be put to shame. And it shall come to pass afterward that I will pour out My Spirit on all flesh; your sons and your daughters shall prophesy, your old men shall dream dreams, your young men shall see visions. And also on My menservants and on My maidservants I will pour out My Spirit in those days....And it shall come to pass that whoever calls on the name of the LORD shall be saved. For in Mount Zion and in Jerusalem there shall be deliverance, as the LORD has said, among the remnant whom the LORD calls.
(Joel 2:27–29, 32)

This prophecy was fulfilled when Jesus' followers were baptized with the Holy Spirit at Pentecost and "tongues of fire" rested on each one of them:

When the Day of Pentecost had fully come, they were all with one accord in one place. And suddenly there came a sound from heaven, as of a rushing mighty wind, and it filled the whole house where they were sitting. Then there appeared to them divided tongues, as of fire, and one sat upon each of them. And they were all filled with the Holy Spirit and began to speak with other tongues, as the spirit gave them utterance. (Acts 2:1–4)

In the revelations and visions I have seen, angels seem to be connected with the fire of the Spirit of God. Once I saw a great angel flying in the heavens. He had a scroll in one hand and a bowl of fire in the other. As I watched, he came down to where I was and said, "God wants to put fire upon His children to purge them and to purify them so they can be cleansed." I thought, *Glory to God, hallelujah!* My prayer is, "How I thank You for the fire, God, and the purging and the cleansing. Anoint us with the fire of the Holy Spirit, Father."

God is sending His fire to purge His children and to take the old leaven (sin and disobedience) out of those who will allow Him. First Corinthians 5:7–8 says,

Purge out the old leaven, that you may be a new lump, since you truly are unleavened. For indeed Christ, our Passover, was sacrificed for us. Therefore let us keep the feast, not with old leaven, nor with the leaven of malice and wickedness, but with the unleavened bread of sincerity and truth.

As I relate these stories of angels in action, God continues to open my eyes. I'm beginning to learn more fully what it means to experience the ministry of angels. I have seen angels being dispatched all over the earth with God's fire. They put it in people who were open to God.

One night, I was preaching at a women's convention, and I had about twenty minutes to finish my message before I had to leave for the airport. Suddenly, God gave me a vision of about seven women in the congregation, and they were all full of fire. As I watched, they turned into skeleton-like forms, and I could see hell beneath them. I said to the congregation, "Let us pray." Immediately, we stood to our feet to pray. As I began to seek God, I related the vision I had seen, and the women ran to the altar and got saved.

Remember, this happened just twenty minutes before I was to leave. Naturally, those leading the convention would have continued the meeting after I left and would have given an altar call. But God wanted that altar call done then, at that time!

Lately, I have been seeing much of the fire of God. I see it in church services—fire around people and on people. Heat from the power of almighty God is "burning out" diseases and sicknesses, such as cancer. I have witnessed angels with bowls of fire, and I have seen them pouring this fire on people. Often, I hear people say, "I feel hot. I feel heat," as they are ministered to by the Lord. Because of this, I have been seeking more understanding about the fire of the Holy Spirit.

A Fire of Judgment

One thing I have learned is that God's fire is one of judgment as well as one of cleansing and healing. In chapter five, we saw that the angels have a role in executing God's judgment in the world. In the Old Testament, God announced through the prophet Amos that He would send fire *"upon the wall of Gaza"* (Amos 1:7), *"upon the wall of Tyre"* (v. 10), and *"upon Teman"* to *"devour the palaces of Bozrah"* (v. 12). *"This is what the Sovereign LORD showed me,"* the prophet further declared. *"The Sovereign LORD was calling for judgment by fire"* (Amos 7:4 NIV). The same fire of purification that brings us joy, peace, and healing will punish the wicked and bring His judgment on them. This fire is from heaven and will fulfill its intended purpose. We all must wake up to this truth. God means what He says.

Once, when I was in prayer, God permitted me to see into the heavenlies. I saw what looked like a rope of fire—it was always aflame—and the angels used it as a measuring line. It reminds me of when the prophet Amos saw a plumb line in the hand of the Lord. (See Amos 7:7–8.) A plumb line has a weight at one end and is used to measure whether a wall is completely straight up and down. The plumb line was a symbolic way of showing that God was measuring the lives of the Israelites to see if they were spiritually upright.

Similarly, I believe that God's judgment is with us today. I really believe that God has, in effect, dropped a plumb line from heaven to separate the righteous from the wicked. We need to be devoted to God with all our hearts. God says, *"I will make justice the measuring line, and righteousness the* [plumb line]*"* (Isaiah 28:17).

Judgment has been going on for quite a while. God wants us to turn to Him before it is too late. How would your life measure up before God? Too many times, the devil brings a spirit of distraction to keep us from hearing the truth. Our lives can be measured as straight and sound only as we receive the Lord Jesus Christ and His righteousness through the atonement He provided for us when He died on the cross, and as we remain in His righteousness through faith and obedience to Him. We are not to take sin lightly.

Not long ago, I was awakened during the night, and I saw a mighty revelation of a huge angel. He had a large scroll in his hands, which he kept turning. Then he opened up the scroll, unrolling it from both ends. The angel looked at me and said, "Thus saith the Lord: The archives of time are opened in heaven." He repeated this three times and then flew away.

I began to seek God about what this meant. The Holy Spirit brought to my mind thoughts about the judgment that has been established for the earth. We are in a time like we have never had before. Yet with troubles and the judgments of God in the land, we are also seeing a mighty outpouring of His Spirit. Again, God does not want people to experience judgment, but to repent and turn to Him through Christ.

Let us allow Him to purge us with that fire and to cleanse us by His holy Word. Many times, in prayer, I have seen God's angels using this plumb line full of fire. I read a book by another person who had seen heaven, and the writer also saw this plumb line on fire. God is drawing the plumb line, saints. We need to get ready for the coming of the Lord.

A Period of Grace

I have seen some ministers and preachers who have preached the Gospel of Jesus Christ and done His will, but who have then fallen into adultery or some other sin. I have noticed that God will give them a space of time to repent, a period of grace. God deals with them, and the angels try to get them back on the right way.

Conviction grips the erring ones' hearts, but if they resist, they start to harden their hearts. In the beginning, they had the glory of the Lord around them. They had the fire of God in them and about them. This fire was like a hedge of protection for them, but as they fell into the errors of sin and lies, they allowed openings to be created in that protection. Their falling into sin also created openings in their anointing from God, and, pretty soon, they became corrupt, with the enemy attacking them every way he could. They became filled with lies and sin.

Yet God's grace still deals with them. He still draws them toward Himself. God's mercy is still calling; He desires them to repent and turn back to Him. Thankfully, many do repent and return to God and His true anointing.

I believe that the revelation God gave me of hell was for a purpose. I am convinced that God gave me the things I have seen and heard so that, as I go and tell them to others, scales will come off people's eyes, and the light of the Gospel will come in. For if they continue in their sins, essentially rejecting Christ, and then die, they will go to hell.

Yet Jesus was manifested to deliver us from sin and save us from eternal punishment. He came to the earth to keep us from a burning hell. Saints, I'm telling you now, we're serving a mighty God who loves us and cares about us.

How Will You Respond?

God's fire is for renewal and judgment. With it, He refreshes and revives His people and punishes the wicked. How will you respond to God's fire? Allow God to purify you and renew you in His love and truth as you *"serve the living and true God, and...wait for His Son from heaven, whom He raised from the dead, even Jesus who delivers us from the wrath to come"* (1 Thessalonians 1:9–10).

9

Angels and Deliverance

n times of danger and distress, the Lord has impressed upon me, *"Call upon Me in the day of trouble; I will deliver you, and you shall glorify Me"* (Psalm 50:15). Many times, I've called upon the Lord *"in the day of trouble."* I've prayed in the Holy Spirit for hours, and the Scriptures have become real and powerful to me. The Lord has said to me, "No matter what you see, no matter what you feel, you must believe in My Word. Believe in what I have promised you. My promises are true." Here are some promises of deliverance from God's Word that we can fill our hearts and minds with and use as the basis of our prayers:

> *Like birds flying about, so will the LORD of hosts defend Jerusalem. Defending, He will also deliver it; passing over, He will preserve it.* (Isaiah 31:5)

> *Even to your old age, I am He, and even to gray hairs I will carry you! I have made,*

and I will bear; even I will carry, and will deliver you. (Isaiah 46:4)

"Do not be afraid of their faces, for I am with you to deliver you," says the LORD. (Jeremiah 1:8)

[Christel] *has made* [you] *alive together with Him, having forgiven you all trespasses, having wiped out the handwriting of requirements that was against us, which was contrary to us. And He has taken it out of the way, having nailed it to the cross. Having disarmed principalities and powers, He made a public spectacle of them, triumphing over them in it.* (Colossians 2:13–15)

And the Lord will deliver me from every evil work and preserve me for His heavenly kingdom. (2 Timothy 4:18)

The Lord knows how to deliver the godly out of temptations. (2 Peter 2:9)

There are many wonderful assurances of God's deliverance in the book of Psalms, as well. Here are several of them:

The LORD is my rock and my fortress and my deliverer; my God, my strength, in whom I will trust; my shield and the horn of my salvation, my stronghold. (18:2)

You are my hiding place; You shall preserve me from trouble; You shall surround me with songs of deliverance. (32:7)

I sought the LORD, and He heard me, and delivered me from all my fears. (34:4)

The angel of the LORD encamps all around those who fear Him, and delivers them. (34:7)

Blessed is he who considers the poor; the LORD will deliver him in time of trouble. The LORD will preserve him and keep him alive, and he will be blessed on the earth; You will not deliver him to the will of his enemies. The LORD will strengthen him on his bed of illness; You will sustain him on his sickbed. (41:1–3)

You called in trouble, and I delivered you. (81:7)

Because he has set his love upon Me, therefore I will deliver him; I will set him on high, because he has known My name. He shall call upon Me, and I will answer him; I will be with him in trouble; I will deliver him and honor him. With long life I will satisfy him, and show him My salvation. (91:14–16)

He sent His word and healed them, and delivered them from their destructions. (107:20)

171

God's Presence Brings Deliverance

The presence of the Lord Himself brings us deliverance. In visions God has given me, I have seen angels coming into churches from the outside, usually through the front door that faces the pulpit in many sanctuaries. When Christ was going to come down, they would begin to sweep with their wings—like a huge fan. They would fan the floor, and a royal red carpet would be laid out for Christ to walk upon.

Then I would see the angels form two parallel rows down the middle aisle of the church. The people in the congregation wouldn't be able to see the angels, but the heavenly messengers would lift their trumpets and blow them as if a king or queen were about to arrive. Then I would see a large chariot come to the main doors at the front of the church. Huge angels would open the doors—they were spiritual doors—and Christ would come in.

Oh, my, He was so beautiful! Angels were always with Him to escort Him and bring messages in books and scrolls. Some of the angels carried horns of fire. Others carried swords or other things.

When Christ would come in, the minister would say, "Oh, I feel the presence of the Lord." I would see clouds appear over the congregation. (Similarly, when I'm preaching in home meetings, often the presence of the Lord will begin to roll in, and I'll see what looks like a mist or a cloud hovering over the people. Many will begin to raise their hands and say, "I feel the presence of the Lord.") It seemed as if there were hundreds of angels working with the Lord. They also worked with the ministers to bring the healing of Jesus to people, and they worked when prophecy was given. Through all this, I knew God was telling me that angels are with us.

I have seen this mighty vision many, many times during my travels over the past ten years. Whenever I see it, souls are always saved. There is such a great move of God that people repent of their sins when I preach on hell. I see the angels go to work in the congregation, and sometimes I see people who are bound in chains, really black chains. The angels torch the chains with fire as the people repent before God. I see people forgiving completely those who have hurt them. They raise their hands and praise the mighty King of kings and Lord of lords.

During these mighty visitations, the Lord will get out of His chariot and walk through the church. He will touch certain people on the head. The anointing of God, the covenant of God, is so real! Believe that Jesus died to make us whole. Believe that He is coming back. Believe that He will manifest His glory in our services if we will let him, if we will believe Him.

Satan wants to cause us to doubt in order to hinder us. He wants to interject unbelief into all of us. Yet hallelujah, our God has paid the price for our deliverance! Our Lord Jesus did it for us! If we will only join with Him, if we will only forgive one another, we will receive absolute forgiveness. (See Matthew 6:14–15.) Let there be no blockage in that joining. Let us be healed of our infirmities, our sicknesses, and our diseases.

The Power of the Cross in Deliverance

On another occasion, I was preaching in a church service, and I was under a heavy anointing. Suddenly, I saw a vision of angels carrying a huge white cross across the front of the church. As the people were prayed for by another minister, I could see power come out of the end of the cross and go onto the person being prayed for. Each one was healed or delivered as they were touched by the power coming from the cross.

I have seen the same thing many other times. As I preach the living Word of God, I can see the cross over my head. Power always comes from the cross. It is through the power of the Cross that deliverance is accomplished and salvation is possible. We can be delivered today if we will only claim for ourselves what Jesus Christ paid for on Calvary. The secret is in the Atonement. We must believe in Jesus, and we must believe in His miracles.

Again, one of the greatest tricks of the devil is to bring doubt and unbelief to us. God wants to bring us joy, happiness, and fulfillment, but the devil wants to bring us pain, sorrow, and grief. God is greater than all these things, however, and we must look to Him. Deliverance is possible through the power of the Cross.

God's Compassion Leads to Deliverance

I was flying on an airplane one day, thinking about a crisis someone in my family was having, when I started crying, and the tears began to flow down my face. Thank the Lord, I had some privacy: I was wearing sunglasses, and there weren't many people in the section of the plane I was in. It was a long flight, so I just curled up in the corner next to the window as I wept.

As the tears streamed down my face, I looked out the window and was amazed to see a beautiful rainbow! Immediately, I remembered the promises of God. When He put the first rainbow in the sky, He promised Noah that He'd never destroy the earth with a flood again. (See Genesis 9:8–17.) Seeing the rainbow that day encouraged my heart because I was reminded of the precious promises of God.

Then, as if affirming what I had seen in nature, I saw a beautiful, glorious, overwhelming vision. I saw what appeared to be a huge red fire in the sky and a resemblance of God on His throne. It is difficult to describe what I saw next, but it looked like a trail leading from the earth up to God's throne. There, in the trail, I saw tears, and immediately I thought of Jesus.

My thoughts of Jesus coincided with my memory of a historical event. In one of the saddest episodes of American history, some of the Cherokee Indians were taken from their land, herded into makeshift forts with minimal facilities and food, then forced to march a thousand miles. (Some made part of the trip by boat in equally horrible conditions.)

About four thousand Cherokee people died during this removal from the Southeast to government reservations in Oklahoma Territory. The route they traveled and the journey itself became known as "The Trail of Tears." The literal meaning of the Cherokee words *Nunna daul Tsuny* is "The trail where they cried."

When I saw this vision of the throne and the trail of tears leading to it, I thought of this historical event, but my most vivid thoughts were of Jesus. I remembered how Jesus walked the *Via Dolorosa,* the Way of Sorrow, climbing up that hill to Calvary. I remembered the tracks of God, the pain and suffering. Then I remembered the pain, suffering, and sorrow that the saints of God still go through at times. As a sign that He was with me, God gave me a poem that I call "In the Tracks of God's Tears."

In the tracks of God's tears were many
written words,
Many messages unto God of sorrow and
grief.
In the tracks of these tears, the enemy
has done great harm.
To many people on the earth, he's
inflicted great harm.
The tracks of these tears are cries unto God
Mixed with doubt and unbelief of God's
covenant promise.
Such sorrow, such grief of heart as, you see,
The enemy kills and wounds our children,
And others we love.
But yet there's hope in the tracks of
God's tears.
Yet there's life, there's peace, in the
tracks of God's tears.

As I continued looking out the window, it seemed as if tears were falling from heaven. Each teardrop had a divine message in it, leaving a trail down to the earth. I knew that God had heard my cries; He is truly touched by the things we go through.

There are many stories in the tracks of God's tears. His teardrops come down like rain and mix with our tears. My tears and yours are a language unto God.

You number my wanderings; put my tears into Your bottle; are they not in Your book?

177

When I cry out to You, then my enemies will turn back; this I know, because God is for me. In God (I will praise His word), in the LORD (I will praise His word), in God I have put my trust; I will not be afraid. What can man do to me?

(Psalm 56:8–11)

The revelation that day gave me even greater respect for what Jesus went through and for the love of our great God. He loves us so much that He sent His Son Jesus to give us life eternal so that we may never die. Yet while we are on this earth, we have to continue to tear down Satan's kingdom through the Word of God. We have to continue to do the things that God would have us to do.

The vision also gave me unbelievable joy. Through it, God dried my tears, reminding me that *"surely He has borne our griefs and carried our sorrows"* (Isaiah 53:4). He assured me that my relatives could be set free, and so can you and yours. *"Believe on the Lord Jesus Christ, and you will be saved, you and your household"* (Acts 16:31).

When the plane landed, I continued on to my destination strengthened in the Lord. That night, I ministered at a service where I saw many hurting and sad people. I gave them words of comfort, encouragement, and hope in the Word of the living God. I told them that, truly, the tears

Christ shed for us are as powerful today as they were the day He shed them.

You, too, have probably cried many tears because you have not understood some of the things that have happened to you. Just remember that we can never understand everything in this life. But the holy Word was written to us and given to us by God. The Holy Spirit inspired men of old to write the Scriptures. (See 2 Peter 1:20–21.) Believe it—believe all of it! *"Jesus Christ is the same yesterday, today, and forever"* (Hebrews 13:8). He is the One we are to look to. He is the One we can have hope in. He is the One who gives us delight and joy.

I challenge you today to be encouraged and to know that there is a God who is always taking care of you and your family. He sends His angels to watch over you. They are always ready to work for you and to help you. Be aware of angels and know that they have been sent to you by God.

Cries for Deliverance

In an earlier chapter, we saw that angels fight against the devil on God's behalf. God employs His angels to deliver people from demons, sickness, and disease. In many deliverance services, I have heard people cry out, "God, help me. God, set me free." It was obvious that they really desired deliverance. As they cried out to God, I would see angels appear and firmly touch their hearts. I could see things, or objects, break off the people, and evil spirits would actually come out of their mouths. The angels would bind these evil spirits with chains and take them to the "dry places." (See Matthew 12:43–45.) I have seen some evil spirits shoot through the roof and disappear; others seem to burst into flames.

One night, I was praying diligently in the Holy Spirit for God to deliver people from drugs. From midnight until 6:00 A.M., I interceded with God because I was determined not to rest until I received an answer from Him. Early the next morning, God sent an angel to give me a vision.

As I was caught up in the Spirit, I saw beams of light shoot like arrows from my home straight into heaven. Then I saw the gates of heaven open up, and I saw an army of huge horses. The backs of the horses were approximately four feet wide, and their hooves were about a foot wide. These majestic animals were pure white in color and had skin like satin. They were beautiful, and they were outfitted in armor, ready for battle.

Then I saw those who were riding the horses. They were angels who looked as if they were twelve feet tall or even taller. They were very broad shouldered and wore what looked like big army boots. Pieces of a metal-like substance were strapped around their knees and shins, covering the lower half of their legs. From their waists to their knees, they wore long garments of metal. They had on breastplates of iron, and their sleeves were made of material I have never seen before, but which looked like silver mixed with gold. Each angel had a large sword hanging at his side. Flames shot out from the bottoms and tops of the swords. The angels also wore fierce-looking helmets. Their faces were covered, but there were holes in the helmets that they could see through. Fire came from their mouths, and their eyes were flames of fire. If you saw them on earth, you might think the devil was coming after you; however, I knew that they were coming from heaven to help us.

These angel warriors were riding in formation, rank upon rank, just like an earthly army that is getting ready for battle. It was obvious that they were prepared. Stern-faced and powerful, the angels headed straight for the earth on those mighty horses.

When they reached the earth, the Lord showed me a vision of the horses and riders going into the cities. They rode into the nighttime streets where the drug dealers, murderers, prostitutes, gay bars, and nightclubs were—the streets of pain and sorrow. I saw them go into homes and other places where people were being tormented spiritually. At first, I prayed in alarm, "Oh, my Lord!" Then it occurred to me that they were going in with a powerful deliverance, not a fierce judgment. I saw them walk up to people on the street who were spiritually bound and who didn't even know the angels were there.

On the bound people, I could see spirits—dark shapes, like monkeys or demons. The evil tormentors had wings on their shoulders. Around their heads or their bodies were serpents. What I was seeing was real people who were being attacked by invisible evil spirits.

I saw the warrior angels go up to the evil spirits and cast off the serpents. The angels then seemed to turn the evil spirits into ashes—fire came out of the angels' hands and appeared to cremate the demons. The angels would also touch some of the street people's heads and pull oppressive, evil-looking things off them. I knew they were unclean spirits. The people would shake their heads in relief right there on the street as they were being delivered.

I saw the warrior angels do these things in many locations. For example, I watched the angels go into a place that looked like a nightclub. They went to a man who was sitting in a bar and crying because he had a dark spirit on his shoulder. An angel jerked the monster off him (it was bigger than the man himself), and the thing was turned into ashes. The man shook his head, dried his tears, stood up, and walked out the door. The Holy Spirit said to me,

A change is coming. A deliverance is coming. I am delivering many from the trickery and bondage of sin and Satan. You will see a big move of my Spirit in the lands, and I will deliver many through the prayers of the saints. I am anointing you for this ministry because you've been crying out to Me for the deliverance of the people. I will do this thing for you.

Then I saw the angels go into hospitals and other places, delivering people from sicknesses and diseases. It was awesome to see the mighty works of these warrior angels. Demons fled from them. They trembled because they knew they were being destroyed.

For several weeks, I saw this as a recurring vision. I'd be caught up in it and see the angels and the Word. The Bible would open up at times—I would see the scrolls—as the angels worked with the Word of God and the Holy Spirit.

God showed me that, all over the world, deliverance had come in the name of the Son, the Lord Jesus Christ. What an awesome sight it was!

In her book *Marching Orders for the End Battle,* Corrie ten Boom wrote about an experience in the Congo during a rebel uprising that further illustrates how God sends angels to deliver His people:

> When the rebels advanced on a school where two hundred children of missionaries lived, they planned to kill both the children and teachers. Those in the school knew of the danger and therefore went to prayer. Their only protection was a fence and a couple of soldiers, while the enemy, who came closer and closer, amounted to several hundred. When the rebels were close by, suddenly something happened: they turned around and ran away! The next day the same thing happened, and again on the third day. One of the rebels was wounded and was brought to the mission hospital. While the doctor was busy dressing his wounds, he asked him: "Why did you not break into the school as you planned?" "We could not do it. We saw hundreds of soldiers in white uniforms and we became scared." In Africa soldiers never wear white uniforms, so it must have been angels. What a wonderful thing that the Lord can open the eyes of the enemy so that they see angels! We, as children of God, do not need to see them with our human eyes. We have the Bible and faith, and by faith we see invisible things.

Streams of Deliverance

In another revelation God gave me, the Holy Spirit came like a divine wind. He began to flow through towns and cities. As the wind blew, balls of fire began to appear, going up and down and sweeping all over. It was as if the Holy Spirit was preparing the way for something.

Then I saw what looked like large doors opening up into heaven, and I could feel the power of God coming through the doors. It seemed as though the doors were in the universe and heaven was high above them. Through the doors came angels on horses dressed for battle—just as I described earlier. Here again came those spiritual warriors from heaven, full of God's glory, power, might, and majesty!

The angels rode over the land where the wind of the Holy Spirit had flowed, and I could see rivers of white and light and glory moving along. These rivers would move through the mountains and the valleys—they were little rivers and streams of deliverance. Everywhere they flowed, demons by the seeming millions would run away, trying to escape from them. Evil spirits were running and running, and as they ran, fire came out of the angels' swords and appeared to cremate them.

God's Word confirms that the wicked will be consumed. Again, in Malachi 4:3, God says, *"You shall trample the wicked, for they shall be ashes under the soles of your feet.*" I firmly believe that God has to send us delivering angels from heaven because of the abundance of attacks we face from Satan and his cohorts.

Staying Delivered

In one service where miracles were taking place, a young man who was about twenty-five years old came into the service crying. He had a wild and desperate look on his face. You could tell he had been drinking and was high on drugs. He said to me, "Please, please help me. Won't someone help me? I want to be delivered so badly. I'm tired of this life; I'm tired of this addiction. Help me. Help me!"

The compassion of the Lord swept over the room. Filled with this compassion, we began to pray for the young man and to cast out evil spirits from him in Jesus' name. We anointed him with oil. Then we led him in the sinner's prayer, and immediately he began to shake his head. He was totally set free; when he stood up, his eyes were completely clear. This young man raised his hands in the air. Soon, he began to magnify and praise the Lord. God had totally transformed him in about fifteen minutes!

Then a little twelve-year-old boy came over and said to him, "Can I tell you something? Do you know what I saw as the people were praying for you?"

The man answered, "No."

"I saw when the demons left you, and they were standing around, trying to go back into you. But all the people were around you, praying. Then I saw an angel with a sword come and chase them away. They couldn't come back!"

The young man praised the Lord, and we were so happy that God had reached out and saved and delivered him. This man is now with good Christian people and is going to church.

God has revealed many things to me about deliverance. Some of the people we have prayed for truly wanted deliverance, but six weeks later, they had the same demons of lust or addiction. We have to continue to pray for them. We also have to counsel them. We have to teach them that, after a person is delivered, he can't be involved any longer with the things that bound him in the first place.

If you want to taste the goodness of God and the world at the same time, there is a fatal conflict in your heart that has to be resolved. It is very important to stay delivered after God has changed you. Find a good church that believes in Jesus Christ and His deliverance. Obey the Word of God. Keep away from those sinful things that drag you down. Stay close to the heart of God.

These truths are essential because, if you have been delivered, you want to stay delivered!

You have to make up your mind which way you are going. Do you really want to adore Jesus and serve Him? Or do you want to follow the things of the world and the devil? If you have been set free from evil things, God brings you to a place where you have to choose.

God is truly a deliverer, and those whom the Lord delivers are delivered, indeed. (See John 8:36.) Therefore, when you cast out Satan, say, "Satan, you must go in the name of Jesus." When demons are cast out of people, angels stand with chains ready to drag these evil powers away. But there is something we must do for the Lord as we commit our lives afresh to Him.

He expects us to worship Him, to serve Him, to praise Him, and through every situation to believe that He will bring us out. I know and believe that He will. Every minister of the Gospel should believe this. When we do, Jesus will go through the lands demonstrating His power. The Holy Spirit will come and, with the angels, will minister in every service to those who really love God and keep His commandments. You will see a move of God in the lands like you have never seen before.

God is preparing a people for this end-time movement. He is looking for a people who will simply trust Him and love Him for who He is and who will believe what the Word says. I fully believe that God is getting ready to do some really great and mighty things in our lands.

The Anointing Destroys the Yoke

One time, during a service when many people were coming up for prayer, I began to see, in the Spirit, a white light mixed with black in a circle around the seekers' necks. I knew that this circle represented a bondage. The Lord spoke to me and said, "I'm going to break the yoke; the anointing shall destroy the yoke." Then I remembered that the Bible says, *"It shall come to pass in that day that...the yoke shall be destroyed because of the anointing"* (Isaiah 10:27 KJV).

As the people repented of their sins and asked God to forgive and help them, I could see the angels go to work. With their hands, they broke the yokes of bondage right off the people's necks. Serving Satan causes spiritual bondage as well as natural bondage. The people had been under spiritual bondage because they had been serving sin and the devil.

The angels of God do His will and break these yokes through the Word of God and in the power of the Spirit of God. The reason people say, "I feel lighter; I feel better," after they are prayed for is that their bondage has been broken in the spiritual realm. When you get serious with God, when you are real and open before Him, He delivers you. He sets you free!

The main thing is to stay honest in your soul before Him. Second, be sure to forgive other people for any wrongs they have committed against you. By the Word of God, you must forgive anyone who has harmed you and hurt you. Unforgiveness is a horrible thing. You *must* forgive so that the heavenly Father can forgive you. Jesus said in Matthew 6:14–15,

> *For if you forgive men their trespasses, your heavenly Father will also forgive you. But if you do not forgive men their trespasses, neither will your Father forgive your trespasses.*

Deliverance from Satan's Control

Once I was going to another country, and I knew the people in that land worshiped many false gods and idols. However, I also knew that God loved the souls of the people there and wanted to save them. While I was there, the Holy Spirit anointed me to prophesy against their idols and their witchery. I knew, and prophesied, that God's presence and His Word had come into the country to save to the uttermost. (See Hebrews 7:25.) He had come to set the captives free, to undo the heavy burdens, and to take the "scales" off people's eyes so they could receive God's truth. (See Isaiah 61:1; Acts 9:1–18.)

In the spiritual realm, God permitted me to see many faces whose eyes had been shut and whose ears had been closed. Then I saw a visible outline of hands pulling layers of scales off these eyes and ears. Those who were delivered would shake their heads in freedom. They would shout with joy and say, "Oh, I see now. I understand now." It was as though a darkness had blinded their minds, but when God touched them, the blindness that Satan had put there was removed. I knew this vision meant that the Gospel was to go forth to every nation and every country.

In this same country, a pastor's wife and I prayed for many hours over two days. In the middle of the night, I saw a vision of a cart rolling through the city. Everywhere it rolled, it would cut off the heads of thousands of snakes that were stretched out all along the way. As the cart went through the valley killing the snakes, I prayed to God and saw the moving of the Holy Spirit.

Suddenly, it was as if the gates of heaven itself opened up. Armies of angels came sweeping down in majesty. I could see manifestations of the power, the glory, and the might of God. He had sent His angels to earth to deliver the city!

Then I saw the angels go into an opening in the earth. From the darkened depths, they pulled out a round, ugly monster with a horrible-looking head. First they chained the monster; then they began to uproot it. This thing was miles long and had wrapped up the entire city. It had permeated the earth, the streets, the houses, and the atmosphere. But the monster was helpless against the power of God. I watched the angels delivering the city from this evil force for what seemed like hours, and I knew God had liberated the city completely from demon powers.

I told my friend, "You should see what God is doing for this country." Since then, we have heard many good reports of the Gospel moving in that nation. Wonderful things are happening, and churches are being established. But God in His mercy dealt with the devils first and delivered that country from the demon of idolatry and the worship of idols. God says the following in His Word:

> *By the blessing of the upright the city is exalted, but it is overthrown by the mouth of the wicked.* (Proverbs 11:11)

> *Righteousness exalts a nation* [or city], *but sin is a reproach to any people.* (Proverbs 14:34)

> *It is an abomination for kings to commit wickedness, for a throne is established by righteousness. Righteous lips are the delight of kings, and they love him who speaks what is right.* (Proverbs 16:12–13)

> *The LORD will enter into judgment with the elders of His people and His princes: "For you have eaten up the vineyard; the plunder of the poor is in your houses."* (Isaiah 3:14)

God will answer the prayers and intercession of those who are devoted to Him, and He will uproot the evil that is present in their communities and nations.

The Power of Jesus' Name

Something that I have come to expect, but which still constantly amazes me, is the reaction of evil angels—demon spirits—when I rebuke them in Jesus' name. As I have cast out devils in Jesus' name, I have seen angels open up the Bible and shove it in Satan's face; the Word of God becomes a sword that goes after him. I've seen Satan when he looked like a serpent, I've seen him when he looked like a man, and I've seen him when he looked like an angel in disguise. Whatever form he takes, I always recognize that it is the devil. When God's servant or the angels begin to speak the Word of God, the devil backs up and releases his victim. He goes because God's Word stands against him.

It's important for us to have an honest and close relationship with the Lord before we cast out demons in Jesus' name. In the Bible, the sons of Sceva attempted to use the name of the Lord without having a true relationship with Him:

Some of the itinerant Jewish exorcists took it upon themselves to call the name of the Lord Jesus over those who had evil spirits, saying, "We exorcise you by the

Jesus whom Paul preaches." Also there were seven sons of Sceva, a Jewish chief priest, who did so. And the evil spirit answered and said, "Jesus I know, and Paul I know; but who are you?" Then the man in whom the evil spirit was leaped on them, overpowered them, and prevailed against them, so that they fled out of that house naked and wounded. This became known both to all Jews and Greeks dwelling in Ephesus; and fear fell on them all, and the name of the Lord Jesus was magnified. (Acts 19:13–17)

Jesus' name is not a gimmick. He is our powerful Savior, and He is worthy to be worshiped and honored. His name is not to be used lightly. Yet when we use Jesus' name with true reverence and faith, Satan cannot stand against it.

God Has the Victory

It is very important to remember in regard to deliverance that Satan is only a created being. He is neither omnipotent, omniscient, nor omnipresent, as God is. Our Lord Jesus Christ is *always* stronger than the devil or any of his demons. *"Jesus Christ...has gone into heaven and is at the right hand of God, angels and authorities and powers having been made subject to Him"* (1 Peter 3:21–22).

In addition, God has multitudes of angels to carry out His works and plans. Regardless of how many demons the devil has, God's holy angels are more in number. God always has the victory, and He will bring deliverance. *"The LORD is my rock and my fortress and my deliverer; my God, my strength, in whom I will trust; my shield and the horn of my salvation, my stronghold"* (Psalm 18:2).

10

Angels and Prayer

n this chapter, I want to mention two areas in which the angels are involved in our prayers: in our worship and in our intercession. When we understand the activity of angels in answer to our prayers, we will be encouraged to pray and intercede on behalf of ourselves, our families, and others who need God's help and deliverance.

Angelic Activity in Worship

First, the angels join us in worshiping the Lord. The Bible says,

> *Praise the LORD! Praise the LORD from the heavens; praise Him in the heights! Praise Him, all His angels; praise Him, all His hosts! Praise Him, sun and moon; praise Him, all you stars of light! Praise Him, you heavens of heavens, and you waters above the heavens! Let them praise the name of the LORD, for He commanded and they were created.* (Psalm 148:1–5)

In the visions and revelations God has given me, I have seen the activity of angels as God's people worship Him. For example, I have seen the following vision many times during church services. As different groups of people come to worship and praise God, I have watched as the Holy Spirit has moved over the congregation. Suddenly, above the pulpit and behind the choir area, high and between curtains, I will see a large door in a wall. Through the door will come rows of angels with fluttering wings. They are dressed in glistening white garments.

Dozens of angels sweep through the door and look over the situation. It is so beautiful and awesome to see these angels in action. They hold something in their hands, and with it they fan the air as if they are cleansing it. Then a great cloud appears, and on the cloud is the throne of God. The brilliant white throne has glowing colors all around it.

I have also seen this likeness of the throne of God suspended in the air behind the pulpit where an anointed minister was preaching. Angels on both sides of the servant of God would write down what the preacher was saying, what he was doing, and how he or she prayed for the people. Everything was recorded.

On one occasion, I had been to London, England, with my sister to preach the Gospel. When we were returning on the airplane, I was very tired because I had ministered in a number of churches and we had had to deal with many people, some who were Christians and some of who were not. It was a long flight back home, and I was totally exhausted, so I fell asleep.

As I slept, I was suddenly transported into the heavenlies. I could see what appeared to be a large ballroom with curtains such as I had never seen before. The curtains formed a huge circle, and the tops of them were pulled up, like you would hold up a balloon. The bottoms of the curtains were suspended, swinging in the air.

The front of the curtains opened up, and inside I could see scenery. In this ballroom, there were crystal chandeliers, but nothing was holding them up. They just hung in the air. Then I could hear music that was accompanying praise. I could see that worship was taking place. As the front of the drapes opened up, I saw that people and angels were sitting at tables inside and carrying on conversations.

Excitedly, I thought, *O, God, these things were never dreamed of. They are things I never even thought of.* It seemed that redeemed believers and angels were praising God and enjoying fellowship together. Splendor and glory and riches were everywhere. I thought, *Oh, my God is so unique. He is so wonderful,* and I began to praise Him.

One day, in prayer, I had a vision of heaven's throne room with Jesus sitting on the throne.

He was no longer suffering and bleeding, as He had been on the cross; instead, He was being worshiped by what seemed to be millions of angels. The throne He was sitting on was enormous and beautiful. Jesus was dressed in marvelous royal apparel that had long, full sleeves and was interwoven with pure gold and silver. A robe made of another piece of material was draped around His shoulders. It was the most beautiful garment I have ever seen, and it had a wide sash on it.

When I looked up at Christ's face, I saw that He was wearing a crown mixed with green, red, and gold velvet. Diamonds, sapphires, and other jewels glittered all over the crown. I thought, *O my Lord, how beautiful!*

Jesus had a scepter lying across His lap, which He gently tapped with His hand. Fire was on the end of the scepter. Jesus was looking intently at me and smiling. I was on my knees before Him, lifting up my hands and worshiping Him. Then He took the scepter and touched me on the top of my head, blessing me. I looked up, and He touched my heart with a flame of fire. As the fire warmed my heart, I felt tremendous love for God.

The love! The purity! The wholesomeness! As I bowed and worshiped Him, I began to praise Him with all my heart. I thank Jesus for that mighty visitation with the Lord.

It is important for us to realize that our worship of God is made possible only through sacrifice. We can worship because of Jesus' sacrifice on the cross, through which He has reconciled us to God and restored our relationship with Him. In addition, worship is possible only as we offer the Lord our own sacrifices—sacrifices of praise. *"Therefore by [Jesus] let us continually offer the sacrifice of praise to God, that is, the fruit of our lips, giving thanks to His name"* (Hebrews 13:15). Because of what Jesus has done for us, we can join with the angels and worship Him with joy:

> *Thus says the LORD: "Again there shall be heard in this place...the voice of joy and the voice of gladness, the voice of the bridegroom and the voice of the bride, the voice of those who will say: 'Praise the LORD of hosts, for the LORD is good, for His mercy endures forever.'"*
> (Jeremiah 33:10–11)

Angelic Activity in Intercession

Second, angels are especially near to God's saints when they pray. Remember that angels went to Jesus twice and strengthened Him—and He was praying both times! The Bible gives this teaching from heaven's viewpoint:

> *Then another angel, having a golden censer, came and stood at the altar. He was given much incense, that he should*

offer it with the prayers of all the saints
upon the golden altar which was before the
throne. And the smoke of the incense, with
the prayers of the saints, ascended before
God from the angel's hand.

(Revelation 8:3–4)

Many times, in the spiritual realm, I have seen angels gathering the prayers of God's saints at a church altar. They have taken them and gone straight to heaven, where they have presented their prayers before Jesus and the heavenly Father. One time, I saw stairs going up into heaven, and angels carrying our prayers to God like beams of light. Some of the angels flew and some climbed the stairs; some had wings, and some didn't. In addition, at times, I have been awakened and prompted to pray, and I have seen by my bedside a spiritual being writing in a scroll. The angel would be recording my prayers to take them to heaven.

Besides carrying our prayers to heaven, angels are God's messengers who bring answers to prayers. I often see angels answering the prayers of God's saints. I am going to share with you some of what I have seen because I want you to have the same insight that I have been given regarding the involvement of angels in our intercession.

Angels and Prayer for Salvation

Many times, in visions, I have seen angels come into a church, or another place where I was ministering, carrying spiritual crosses. These crosses were huge and pure white, symbolizing wisdom and power. They also emitted a brilliant light, and some had fire coming out of them. The angels would point these crosses toward a backslider or sinner in the room, and the flames of the Holy Spirit would come out from the crosses and envelop the person, who would begin to shake. Then the individual would get up, come to the altar, and repent.

The angels were working with the Spirit of truth and righteousness to encourage people to give their lives to the Lord. It is always a beautiful thing for me to behold. The Lord has revealed to me that He sends His angels to work with us because of the prayers of mothers, fathers, brothers, sisters, pastors, laymen, evangelists, and teachers.

Seeing God do His work of salvation in the lives of men and women is marvelous, indeed, and His angels are active in promoting this work. I remember asking a neighbor, who is also an intercessor, to pray for my work in a particular city. The neighbor said, "When you preach there, God is really going to save souls in that city."

God gave me a vision that confirmed what He was going to do. I saw the heavens open. A large door in heaven swung wide, and many angels riding on horses began coming down to where I was. They came to prepare the way for the work of God. It excited me to see the workings of God in action. I saw books open up, and I recognized the writings in the books. God was promising success for His work. I often see this same scene when I go into towns for services.

In a service one evening, I was preaching on hell and what God had revealed to me about that place. I told the people how we must get right with the Lord, and the church altar filled with people who came forward for prayer. I saw the glory of the Lord coming down around them; God's arms were stretched out to receive them.

It was such a beautiful scene. Many people don't understand that once you surrender to God, He is right there to help you and encourage you. He who calls you will bring you forth. He loves you so much that He shows His mighty mercy to you.

In one vision God gave me, I saw many angels who held crosses in their hands. They would stand the crosses up by some of the people in the meeting, or they would put the crosses on people's shoulders. There was a huge cross, and I understood it to symbolize Christ's cross.

The people who had been given the crosses began to place them at the base of Christ's cross. In the middle of His cross, there was a brilliant light, and it seemed as though the nearer they got to His cross and the light, the closer they got to God. It pays to seek God's face and continue on with Him!

In the visions, Jesus would often say, "Souls, souls, come forth," and angels would spring into action. They would touch some sincere soul who was seeking God. Some of the people had black bands—indicating sin—fastened around them. As the angels would touch the people, I would see them raise their heads in the service and say, "O God, please forgive me. I'm a thief," or "Forgive me; I'm a liar," and so forth. Then the angels would touch these dark bands of bondage and the bands would burst into flames.

Some of the people's hearts looked as black as coal. But as they confessed their lying, cheating, stealing, adultery, witchcraft, or whatever bondage they were in, the blackness would appear to boil out of their hearts. The angels would touch their hearts, and their hearts would become beautiful and pink. It reminded me of the Scripture, *"Then I will...take the stony heart...and give them a heart of flesh"* (Ezekiel 11:19).

To receive this kind of change in our lives, we must totally repent before God. We have to turn to God with all our hearts, all our minds, all our souls, and all our spirits. We are to do all these things in the name of Jesus.

Angels and Prayer for Healing

About five years after the Lord showed me the revelations of hell and heaven, one of my children—who were all still young—became sick. I had been praying for them, and the Lord began to speak to me, saying,

Child, when I took you into hell, I held your left hand. A few times, you thought I had left you, but I hadn't. I was right there. I revealed to you much of the depths of the torments of hell, but I also gave you a great gift of the working of miracles in your left hand. It is a gift from Me to you, especially for the suffering and grief you are seeing. It is My gift so that you can help others on the earth. When the appointed time comes, I will magnify that gift and manifest it to heal the sick.

Use the gift on your children. Use it and pray for them, and they will be healed.

The gift of the working of miracles is listed in 1 Corinthians 12 along with the other gifts of the Spirit. (See verses 8–10.) I began to exercise the gift that God had given me, and God started to train me in it; later on, I would see angels coming into services to assist me as I ministered in this gift.

God began to tell me many things about what He wanted to do in my ministry with healings, signs, wonders, and miracles. Angels were always there, carrying out the orders of God. When I would see them in my services, I would tell the people, "God wants to heal you," and many people were healed. Signs and wonders continue to be manifested in my services today. I see the Lord doing great and mighty things. He is healing the sick and performing marvelous miracles. I know that the day is coming when God is going to pour out more oil and more power upon me so that I can continue to work for Him, exalt Him, and obey His Word to take the message of the Gospel to others in a greater way.

Let me tell you of two other circumstances in which I have witnessed the angels of God participating in healing. At times, when a servant of God is praying over an infant who is critically ill, I have seen angels with scrolls and pens standing in the room, writing down what the minister is saying. Understand, please, that infants are too young to apply faith in such a situation. The minister exercises faith on the infant's behalf, believing that the child is being healed by God's Word and Spirit. He or she may pray, "In Jesus' name and by Jesus' stripes, this child is healed. I cast out the spirit of infirmity in Jesus' name. Spirit of infirmity, you must go. I take dominion over you in the name of Jesus!" I have seen how, as the minister lays his hands on a child's head and anoints him or her with oil, praying according to God's Word (see James 5:14–15), an angel will place his hands on the afflicted one's little legs. Other angels sometimes just stand there, perhaps in support of the healing.

The second circumstance was a very personal one. On May 3, 2001, my son Scott had a grand mal seizure. At the time, I was in Michigan preaching the Gospel, and I was staying at the home of my sister. I was unaware that Scott had had a major seizure, but I had a vision of angels coming down from heaven and getting ready to do something on the earth. They were mighty, warrior angels. Then, as I was walking up the stairs at my sister's house, I clearly heard the words, *"I am the resurrection and the life"* (John 11:25).

A few hours later, my daughter Teresa called and told me about Scott's grand mal seizure. She said the paramedics had taken him to a hospital, but she didn't know which one. As I tried to find out where my son was, I still did not know the whole story and what a terrible thing had happened to him.

I called some people in Michigan and other states and asked them to pray. A man in Michigan who has the gift of prophecy called me and said, "Mary, I want to tell you what I see. I see your son in a vision, and I see God connecting the soul and the spirit back together in the brain. I see the brain, and I see the Lord healing this child." And he began to prophesy and pray.

This man is a good friend of mine, and when he had finished praying, I said, "Brother, I know that you're a prophet and a man of God, but

I don't really believe Scott's situation was that tragic. I think it was just a normal seizure."

I am telling you this story so you may know how important it is to believe in God and serve Him, to keep His commandments and know that He is the Word of God. He is the Healer and Deliverer. He is the same God *"yesterday, today, and forever"* (Hebrews 13:8).

When I finally contacted Scott, I asked him, "Son, how are you? What has happened to you?" As he began to tell me, he could hardly talk. He said he'd had a horrible seizure and had been in the hospital. He had gotten home about four o'clock that morning. I said, "You need to really praise God that you didn't die."

He said, "Mom, I did die."

"What are you talking about?" I asked. "What happened?"

Scott told me that he had been about to go into a grocery store when, suddenly, he had felt a lot of pain in his shoulder. Right there, he had a seizure, and that was all he remembered. When he woke up, he was in the hospital. The paramedics told him that when they first arrived, he wasn't breathing and showed no vital signs. They said they had brought him back to life with electric shock and other emergency procedures and then taken him to the hospital.

The paramedics were astonished at Scott's good condition because, given the severity of his seizure, he should have been brain-dead and on life-support machines. But by a miracle of God, Scott was raised up—at the very time I heard the voice of God at my sister's house saying, *"I am the resurrection and the life"* (John 11:25). The warrior angels I had seen coming down from heaven in the vision had apparently come to fight for Scott's life.

Angels and Prayer for Miracles

When I lived in Michigan, I led a prayer meeting that met in my home. One day, I was leaving my house to run some errands in town with several believers who had been with me in the prayer meeting, when a storm quickly arose, and rain started pouring down.

As we got into the automobile, the winds and the rain seemed to get worse, so we sat in the car praying in the Spirit. Suddenly, we heard sirens and saw an ambulance. We knew that something had happened, such as an automobile accident, so we proceeded to the store with caution and completed our errands.

We were taking a different route on the way back when we saw another ambulance's light flashing. There had been a car wreck. We saw a stretcher beside the road with someone lying on it. A white sheet covered the victim, so we knew the person was dead. The police pulled us over to wait by the side of the road while they got the other people out of the wreckage. It was still raining hard—just pouring.

As we waited, the Holy Spirit fell on us and impressed us to pray. As we prayed in the Spirit, we began, under the Spirit's direction, to command life to come back into the victim. As the Holy Spirit prompted us, we remitted the person's sins in the name of Jesus. (See John 20:23.) In a few minutes, we saw that white sheet raise up. Then the person on the stretcher lifted up his hands and pulled the sheet away from himself.

All at once, one of the paramedics turned around, saw what was happening, and ran over to work with the injured man. The paramedic was happy because God had put life back into the victim. We never even touched the man, but the angels did. We didn't even get out of the car, but the Word of God was in action to save that person's life.

Angels and Prayer for Deliverance

A few years ago, my family was going through an especially rough time. A family member had disappeared and had not been seen for almost six months. No one could find him. This was one of the most difficult crises my family had ever faced. We had to believe God with everything in us. In addition to this crisis, other blows constantly rained on us. It seemed that the old enemy was hammering us first on one side and then on another.

I'm sure many of you can understand how hard this time was for us because you've gone through similar experiences. Perhaps the devil is hitting your bank account, taking money that doesn't belong to him, and you wonder where it is all going. Maybe he is causing your automobiles to break down or your appliances to stop working. When he isn't doing that, you are getting sued for something. Everything in your life seems to be in an uproar because there is always some problem. That's exactly what we were going through. Troubles and difficulties were constant in our family at that time in our lives. I thought, *O Lord, haven't I prayed enough? Haven't I stood on Your Word enough?* I went to God in prayer because I was so deeply grieved over the situations that were occurring.

During this difficult time, the Lord would send His angels, and His peace would come upon us. God promised us peace, deliverance, and help. (See, for example, John 14:27; Psalm 34:7; Isaiah 41:10, 13–14.) So we began to stand on the Word of God, no matter how hard the waves hit.

One day I would have to be the strong one; the next day I would be weak and one of my children would have to be strong. It was awesome to see God's angels ministering to us. Someone with the gift of prophecy would call me, or a friend would call me, or I would call them, and we would encourage one another in the Lord. It is so important for us to encourage one another, especially during difficult times.

In the midst of this trial, I saw a mighty vision in which God assured me that He is the Deliverer. The vision seemed to last for hours! It was a revelation of how the Lord brings deliverance to the lands through His angels! In the vision, I observed angels going into houses. The houses looked as though they were way back in a forest, and darkness was all around.

Suddenly, I saw witches and warlocks having séances. I also saw devil worshipers. Then I saw the angels of God shake the places where they were. When the angels did this, the witches, warlocks, and devil worshipers ran out of the buildings. They got into their cars and drove away with the fear of the Lord upon them. It was an awesome sight to see.

I have seen this kind of vision many times in the past fifteen years or so. I see it at least twice a year—usually when I am in intercessory prayer. I know that God is the Deliverer and that He sends His angels to His children on errands of mercy. He intervened in the situation my family was going through. Our family member was found and, though he had been ill, God restored him to health!

On another occasion, I had been in deep prayer and meditation. As I ministered at a church service that night, I saw angels everywhere. Every angel had a golden sword in his hand. The Spirit of the Lord spoke clearly to me in an unmistakable voice:

Child, when prayer time comes for the people, I want to heal certain physical problems. I want this to be a sign in your ministry that the testimony of hell that I gave you is true. I have given My word that I will give signs and wonders and work miracles as the Gospel of the Lord Jesus Christ is preached.

I became so excited! In my spirit, I could see an angel with a large book writing things down as I preached. The ceiling seemed to open up, and I could see a vision of the throne of God. Angels were rejoicing all around it and praising God.

When it was time for the altar call, I saw angels going among the congregation, nudging people to go to the altar and give their hearts to the Lord. When the angels touched the hearts of individuals, the blackest sins began to churn up from their hearts as they knelt and prayed to God. It was so beautiful to see God working in their lives!

In the Spirit, I could see chains wrapped around the people. As they received forgiveness, angels seemed to break the bondage, to shatter the chains, to cast them off. The bands broke as people began to raise their hands and confess their sins to the Lord.

Cries and shouts went up all around from souls who were being delivered. It was wonderful. In many of my services all over the world, God provides great miracles like these, and wonderful deliverances happen. I praise God for His signs, wonders, and miracles. I know that the angels are at work helping me with the ministry of the Lord Jesus Christ, which He has given me.

One day, I was in prayer when the Lord began to talk to me about the revelations He was giving to me:

My child, you must learn that many times I will open up a vision to you, and what I'm showing you is not present right there before you. It will be for the future, or it will be happening in another part of the world. You were given the vision so that you can intercede. Listen to Me, and I will give you instructions on how to pray.

Sometimes, people will receive a revelation, and they will think that what is happening is right there beside their beds. They will think that what they are seeing is there in the room with them, but it is not so. I am a holy God, and I am protective of my children. I am revealing truth and mysteries to you so you can reveal them to the world.

I'm showing you one of the workings of the enemy, Satan, so that you can pray; and the blood that I shed—the blood covenant—will come and stop the flow of these channels, these avenues, of the devil.

I was so excited! I said, "Okay, Lord."

Time went by, and one day, I was in Phoenix to preach the Gospel. Some of us had been in intercessory prayer for the city. We had prayed and gone to sleep, but I awoke at three o'clock in the morning. I felt as though I had been awake for hours.

I looked at the ceiling, and I could see something appearing before my eyes. A manifestation of a spiritual object came through the ceiling and hovered around in a circle. At one end of the object, I could see a small opening that measured about eight inches by twelve inches. I saw that the tiny opening was a door.

As I looked through this door, I could see a witch with a crystal ball sitting at a table. I knew that she could see from the crystal ball into the place where I was. I also knew that God had allowed me to see what I was seeing, and that He had allowed her to be able to do this in order to show me how to pray. I took in this whole scenario very quickly. Then the door shut, and the thing moved right out of the room.

I got up and said, "Lord, what in the world was that?" God said to me,

I'm showing you strategy of the devil. Many witches and warlocks work for the devil in this area, and they have these crystal balls. They have figured out how to go through the airways and spy out the land in certain areas where My blood does not provide a covering. A blood covering can be provided only through prayer and through believing in Me and the covenant of God. Many do not believe in My protection as you do.

When My righteousness covers my children and they are living holy lives before Me, when they are doing the best they can, My covenant—the Atonement—stands for them and their families. No matter where they are, no matter where their children are, a hedge of protection surrounds them.

Many do not believe this, but I know you do. I've proven this to you many times over with your own children and your family. Many times, I've saved your family from harmful things that crossed their paths.

My covenant—the atonement for the healing of the body, the blood that I shed over two thousand years ago—still stands today. My covenant promises are for you and your children.

What I'm revealing to you is a message for you to tell to other people. It is to protect the innocent and the guilty. My desire is to save the guilty and weak. I desire this, and this is why I'm telling you these things—so that you can tell the world.

The armlike object you saw, with the opening and a small door at the front of it, was a passageway from the crystal ball through the spirit realm to where you are in this home.

I allowed you to see this hovering in the atmosphere in order to teach you to pray. Watch closely, and I'll show you something else.

God then showed me what looked like a huge television screen. I could see a woman's face, and I would recognize her now if I could see her in the flesh. She was clearly visible, and she was hovering over a crystal ball and screaming in a loud voice. Then the devil came roaring and screaming into the place where she was. "Why did you let her see you?" Satan yelled. "Why did you let her see you?"

The woman and the devil began arguing. This led to fighting and more yelling. I heard the devil tell this wicked woman that she had a big mouth and would tell everybody. The devil—his form was huge—grabbed the wall and started roaring and screaming in anger. Then he went through the door, and the Lord suddenly spoke to me,

> Plead My blood! Plead the blood of Jesus! Plead the blood that I shed. The life and the power of the blood of Jesus that was shed two thousand years ago has never lost its power over situations like these. The blood has power over those crystal balls that are the spirit realm's venues of sin; it can shut those doors.

I did just as the Lord said because I believed Him. When I began to pray, I saw fire mixed with blood. I saw vapors of smoke. I saw the power of God shoot through the atmosphere and explode the woman's crystal ball. She screamed and ran all over the room; as the power of God hit again, she ran out of the room.

The Lord told me, "Pray in every area where I send you as you have just done here. Pray right now for others who have these crystal balls."

So I prayed for a long time. He showed me how to pray. His angels taught me how to pray through the Scriptures, how to bind and loose (see Matthew 18:18), how to plead His precious blood, and how to rely on the Word of God. Every time I would do these things, there would be a great deliverance among the people. In the spiritual realm, I saw the angels scatter many of the enemies of God's people. In one vision, I saw what looked like about ten thousand scattered at one time.

I also saw people delivered who were in supernatural bondage. It was as though ropes and vines had grown around them, but when the fire hit them, the shackles would explode. I knew that God was showing me these mighty revelations through the power of His Holy Spirit. I thought, *God, You are such a wonderful God.*

Then I saw the dove of the Holy Spirit soaring through the heavens. God began to draw people by His Spirit. People started coming to the Lord, and I was so happy and excited to see the blessings and joy of the Lord. I truly began to understand that we are in a spiritual war where good is fighting against evil.

The Prayers of Believers

I thank God for these revelations and for the angels that I have seen. I believe God wants us to understand that the prayers of believers are very important. We are called to pray. Yet we shouldn't pray just once a day and then forget about it. When the Holy Spirit prompts us to pray, we should pray right then, regardless of where we are. Paul taught us to *"pray without ceasing"* (1 Thessalonians 5:17) in the Spirit.

Through the prayers of those who believe His Word, God commissions His angels to come and work with us, and He brings salvation, healing, and deliverance to people. Let the Lord's words to Jeremiah when he was in exile be an encouragement to you as you pray for yourself and others:

For I know the thoughts that I think toward you, says the LORD, thoughts of peace and not of evil, to give you a future and a hope. Then you will call upon Me and go and pray to Me, and I will listen to you. And you will seek Me and find Me, when you search for Me with all your heart. I will be found by you, says the LORD, and I will bring you back from your captivity.

(Jeremiah 29:11–14)

11

The Meaning of Angels

am so grateful that God has anointed me as His servant and has allowed me to see these supernatural visions in order to communicate the message He wants His people to know. I have shared with you only a part of the things I have encountered in the revelations God has given to me. But I want to assure you that the work of God's angels is all found in His Word, and it is wonderful!

The purpose of this book is to encourage you in your faith. The study of angels provides us with a wonderful opportunity to come to know God and His ways better. As we learn about angels, we are not to place our focus on celestial beings themselves but on almighty God and the power and grace He manifests through His servants, the angels. Our knowledge of God's special messengers and how He works through them can help to enlighten our doubts, solidify our beliefs, comfort us in sorrow, and give us peace. The ministry of angels on our behalf reveals that God loves us and is continually working to help us. What a comfort and joy that knowledge is to us!

One of the messages of *A Divine Revelation of Angels* is that God has angels for every need you have. You may not always see them, but God sends His angels to go before you, stand behind you, walk beside you, and be solid ground underneath your feet. There are hosts and legions of angels whom He can send to give you strength or any other blessing you may need. Believe what God says in His Word! He cares about you! *"Casting all your care upon Him, for He cares for you"* (1 Peter 5:7).

Another message of this book is that the Word of God and the angels are always in action accomplishing His purposes. God is continually working out His plan of salvation, redemption, and judgment for the world. He wants us to know this and to participate in His purposes with Him. How can we best do this? The biblical examples of the nature and role of angels and the visions and revelations I have shared with you reveal these important truths, among others, for loving and serving God.

The Importance of Worship

The angels' adoration of God underscores His majesty. Angels are an example to us of how we should reverence and worship God. As all of heaven and the universe echo with the praises of God's angels, let us remember to honor and praise God, too. Heaven gives us this model for our worship:

The four living creatures, each having six wings, were full of eyes around and within. And they do not rest day or night, saying: "Holy, holy, holy, Lord God Almighty, who was and is and is to come!" Whenever the living creatures give glory and honor and thanks to Him who sits on the throne, who lives forever and ever, the twenty-four elders fall down before Him who sits on the throne and worship Him who lives forever and ever, and cast their crowns before the throne, saying: "You are worthy, O Lord, to receive glory and honor and power; for You created all things, and by Your will they exist and were created." (Revelation 4:8–11)

Amen and amen! Blessed be the Lord God Almighty!

The Importance of Believing

Second, learning about the ministry of angels on our behalf should give us confidence in God's love and power and encourage our hearts that God is with us, no matter what we're going through. Let us remember the words of Psalm 91:14–15:

*Because he has set his love upon Me, there-
fore I will deliver him; I will set him on
high, because he has known My name. He
shall call upon Me, and I will answer him.*

We need to trust God in all things and concentrate on loving and serving Him, for He is
worthy of all our trust. Hebrews 11:33–35 encourages us that the saints of Bible times

through faith *subdued kingdoms,
worked righteousness, obtained promises,
stopped the mouths of lions, quenched the
violence of fire, escaped the edge of the
sword, out of weakness were made strong,
became valiant in battle, turned to flight
the armies of the aliens. Women received
their dead raised to life again. And others
were tortured, not accepting deliverance,
that they might obtain a better resurrection.* (emphasis added)

First Peter 1:5 says that we are *"kept by the power
of God through faith for salvation ready to be
revealed in the last time."* Let us exercise that faith
in our daily lives so that we may accomplish all
that God wants to do through us in the ministries
and gifts He's given us to build up His kingdom.

The Importance of Discernment

Today's "angel mania" and the false ideas about
angels that are being circulated in both religious
and nonreligious circles show us the importance of

using discernment when it comes to the use of spiritual gifts and encounters with spiritual beings. We should always remember that the devil is able to transform himself *"into an angel of light"* (2 Corinthians 11:14) in order to deceive us. Therefore, we must fill our hearts and minds with God's Word as we test the spirits.

We should no longer be children, tossed to and fro and carried about with every wind of doctrine, by the trickery of men, in the cunning craftiness of deceitful plotting, but, speaking the truth in love, [we should] grow up in all things into Him who is the head; Christ.   (Ephesians 4:14–15)

Beloved, do not believe every spirit, but test the spirits, whether they are of God; because many false prophets have gone out into the world. By this you know the Spirit of God: Every spirit that confesses ["acknowledges" NIV] that Jesus Christ has come in the flesh is of God, and every spirit that does not confess ["acknowledge" NIV] that Jesus Christ has come in the flesh is not of God. And this is the spirit of the Antichrist, which you have heard was coming, and is now already in the world.   (1 John 4:1–3)

The Importance of Obedience

As I wrote earlier, God wants us to tear down the unclean altars in our lives and make ourselves altars of holiness to Him as we make a new commitment to love and serve Him. This means that we must repent of our sin, come before God in humility, and ask Him to cleanse and restore us through Christ. We must remember that His judgment is going forth in the world. Let us allow Him to discipline us by purging us with His fire and cleansing us by His holy Word.

Once, when I was in prayer, an angel brought me this vision. I saw two huge spiritual faces looking at each other—face-to-face and eye-to-eye. The faces had no bodies; they were just faces. Then, one of the faces kissed the other softly on the lips. I thought of the Word of God: *"Mercy and truth have met together; righteousness and peace have kissed"* (Psalm 85:10). In the book of Psalms, God has much to say about mercy and truth:

> *The LORD is good; His mercy is everlasting, and His truth endures to all generations.* (100:5)

> *But You, O Lord, are a God full of compassion, and gracious, longsuffering and abundant in mercy and truth.* (86:15)

> *Righteousness and justice are the foundation of Your throne; mercy and truth go before Your face.* (89:14)

> *All the paths of the LORD are mercy and truth, to such as keep His covenant and His testimonies.* (25:10)

God shall send forth His mercy and His truth.   (57:3)

Then the angel took me back in time, and the Lord showed me another vision that I had seen years ago. God was sitting on His throne. Now, I didn't see God; I just saw the outline of God. I saw the glory of God and the fire of God and the outline of a form sitting on a large throne somewhere in the universe. In each of His hands—His very large hands—was a large rope and a type of round object.

I couldn't see what the ropes were fastened to, but they were in His hands, and He was trying to pull them together. It was as if a tug-of-war was going on between the two. Every time they nearly met, it seemed as if something would struggle against Him and something would pull the opposites apart. Just as He was getting ready to join them together, an invisible force always opposed Him.

Then I saw faces on the ends of the two round objects, and they were the same faces I had seen in the other vision—mercy and truth. I began to understand that, in this symbolic vision, God was trying to get mercy and truth to meet together in our hearts. God desires us to worship Him with integrity. Jesus said,

But the hour is coming, and now is, when the true worshipers will worship the Father in spirit and truth; for the Father

*is seeking such to worship Him. God
is Spirit, and those who worship Him
must worship in spirit and truth.*

(John 4:23–24)

God wants our hearts and our minds to be
holy and clean. In the vision, the angels seemed
to be encouraging me in this truth. Suddenly,
this Scripture came to me: *"Love the LORD your
God with all your heart, with all your soul, with
all your strength, and with all your mind"* (Luke
10:27). I thought,

> *O Lord, the enemy is planting so much
> unbelief and doubt in Your body all over
> the world. It's almost as if, when You get
> us to join together in the heart, something
> happens to take away some truth or mercy
> You've given us. This is why we've got to
> dig in Your Word and believe Your Word,
> no matter what we get hit with. No matter
> what we think in opposition to Your Word,
> we must go forth and believe Your Word.*

Truly, when mercy and truth meet together,
how precious and wonderful the Lord is! God is
calling you to a special place in Him. As you yield
to Him and live a holy life (see 1 Thessalonians
5:23), He will use you mightily—and His angels
will go with you continuously!

Once I was praying in preparation for
preaching at a service, when I saw many large
angels in the sky. They were working diligently

at some task. It seemed to me that they were pulling a ropelike vine through a door into heaven.

Doors were open in the sky, and the vine went through one of the doors and up onto a table. Many angels were sitting at the long table examining the vine. If they found bad places in it, they would take a big knife and trim off the contaminated part before it did any further damage. I thought of how God prunes us, and I remembered Jesus' words:

> *I am the vine, you are the branches. He who abides in Me, and I in him, bears much fruit; for without Me you can do nothing. If anyone does not abide in Me, he is cast out as a branch and is withered; and they gather them and throw them into the fire, and they are burned. If you abide in Me, and My words abide in you, you will ask what you desire, and it shall be done for you. By this My Father is glorified, that you bear much fruit; so you will be My disciples.*
>
> (John 15:5–8)

The vine of the Lord goes all over the earth. Some people are grafted into it, but some are cut off. It is very important for us to love the Lord and keep His commandments as best we can. It is essential that we obey Him, regardless of what He asks us to do.

Be encouraged in the work of God that you are doing. Knowing that angels are around you to assist and bless you will give you encouragement to hear from God. As you are strengthened in the work of God, He will begin to reveal special things to you. Ministers of the Gospel must believe that while Jesus is working through His Holy Spirit and through manifestations of power, angels are present to minister in the services and to the servants who really love God and keep His commandments.

Obey Him, and you will see a move of God in the land like you have never seen before. God is looking for a people who will love Him enough to obey Him and trust Him for who He is, and who will believe what the Word says. He is preparing just such a people. It is His will that we walk close to Him. God is getting ready to do some really great and mighty things in our lands. We have much work to do before Jesus comes again.

This is the hour for us to get ready for a move of God like we've never had before. The Lord imparts His gifts to His people. He gives freely and liberally to His own. God's precious gifts are for the holy people of God so that they can train others to do the works of the Lord. I believe that He is preparing all who are open to Him, so that they can teach people and help them to understand how much God loves them.

The Importance of Perseverance

God's holy, elect angels persevered in loving and serving Him even when Satan and many other angels rebelled against Him. They are a model for us of everlasting devotion to God and His ways. Let us take their example and persevere in our dedication and loyalty to God and in our work for Him. The Bible assures us that

> *God is not unjust to forget your work and labor of love which you have shown toward His name, in that you have ministered to the saints, and do minister. And we desire that each one of you show the same diligence to the full assurance of hope until the end, that you do not become sluggish, but imitate those who through faith and patience inherit the promises.*
> (Hebrews 6:10–12)

Remember what happened when Jesus battled Satan in a titanic struggle with temptation in the wilderness. Jesus faced His temptation alone, quoted the truth of the Scripture to the enemy, and defeated Satan. It was *then* that the angels came and ministered to Him.

Likewise, you and I often have to face our temptations without any human help. Many times, we do not have anyone to stand with us in the crucial hour. Yet God's Word lets us know that the Lord never leaves us and that, when the battle is won, we will be ministered to by His angels. What a lesson we can learn from this! We do not go through dark days and trying times in vain. God has deliverance for us, and He will send His angels to strengthen and encourage us. Blessed be our God!

The Importance of Prayer

Finally, in chapter ten, we saw the role that angels have in answering our prayers and the importance of our intercession for God's work of salvation and deliverance to go forth. God will deliver many through the prayers of the saints. Paul taught us in Ephesians 6:18 to pray *"always with all prayer and supplication in the Spirit, being watchful to this end with all perseverance and supplication for all the saints."*

Ask the Holy Spirit to guide you in your prayers. Romans 8:26–27 says,

The Spirit also helps in our weaknesses. For we do not know what we should pray for as we ought, but the Spirit Himself makes intercession for us with groanings which cannot be uttered. Now He who searches the hearts knows what the mind of the Spirit is, because He makes intercession for the saints according to the will of God.

Let us seek God's will and ask Him to bring salvation, healing, and deliverance as we intercede for our families, communities, and nations.

The God of Angels and Men

Through our study of angels, we have seen that the Lord of Hosts is a mighty God who accomplishes His purposes in heaven and on earth. The verse that strengthens my heart and can strengthen the heart of every true believer is found in Daniel 4:35: *"He does according to His will in the army of heaven and among the inhabitants of the earth. No one can restrain His hand."* He is the God of both angels and men. He is our God! Let our prayer ever be, *"Your kingdom come. Your will be done on earth as it is in heaven"* (Luke 11:2)!

Notes

Preface

Sir Francis Bacon, *Oxford History of Quotations*, 3rd ed. (Oxford: Oxford University Press, 1980), 27.

Chapter One: Are Angels Real?

Nancy Gibbs, "Angels Among Us," *Time* (December 27, 1993): 56.

Chapter Two: The Truth about Angels

Billy Graham, *Angels: God's Secret Agents* (Nashville: W Publishing Group, 1995), 30.

Chapter Three: What Are Angels Like?

Dr. David Jeremiah, *What the Bible Says about Angels* (Sisters, Ore.: Multnomah Books, 1996), 116.

Herbert Lockyer, *All the Angels in the Bible* (Peabody, Mass.: Hendrickson Publishers, Inc., 1995), 114.

Chapter Six: Angels and Protection

Billy Graham, *Angels: God's Secret Agents* (Nashville: W Publishing Group, 1995), 137–39.

Chapter Nine: Angels and Deliverance

Corrie ten Boom, *Marching Orders for the End Battle* (Fort Washington, Pa.: Christian Literature Crusade, 1969), 112–13.

Part IV

Chapter Questions for Personal Reflection or Group Discussion

Chapter Questions for Personal Reflection or Group Discussion

Chapter One: Are Angels Real?

1. What is your conception of angels? Where did you learn this idea (e.g., church, the Bible, paintings and sculpture, television)?

2. Are the current cultural depictions of angels realistic, fantastical, or both?

3. Do you think angels have a role in your life? If so, what role?

4. Have you (or someone you know) experienced what you considered an angelic visitation? What was it like? What happened?

5. What does Mary Baxter say is the reason she received visions and revelations about angels from God? (pp. 21–23)

Chapter Two: The Truth about Angels

1. (a) Why is it dangerous to study about angels from those who don't have a solid biblical understanding of their true nature and ways? (b) Why is the Bible our best source for understanding the truth about angels? (pp. 25–26)

2. Why shouldn't we worship angels, pray to them, or seek their guidance? (pp. 27–32)

3. When angels help and assist us, where is that help ultimately coming from? (pp. 29, 32)

4. How do we know that Jesus Christ is greater than the angels? (pp. 32–35)

5. In what ways are angels and humans distinct? (pp. 35–39)

6. How can we tell the difference between true angels and demonic beings disguised as angels? (pp. 44–45)

7. What is your best protection against demonic deception and evil? (pp. 45–49)

Chapter 3: What Are Angels Like?

1. List five facets of the nature of angels. (pp. 53–61)

2. What are the qualities of spirit beings? (pp. 54–55)

3. How do angels know and learn about God, His ways, and His plan for humanity? (pp. 58–59)

4. How many angels are there? (pp. 61–64)

5. In what three forms did angels in the Bible appear to humanity? (pp. 66–72)

6. Give two or three biblical examples for each form. (pp. 66–72)

7. Why did the writer of Hebrews tell us we should be hospitable to strangers? How should this knowledge change the way we act toward other people—whether they are acquaintances or strangers? (pp. 71–72)

Chapter Four: Types and Ranks of Angels

1. The Bible indicates that the angelic realm includes at least four holy beings called "_____," "_____," "_____," and "_____." (p. 77)

2. The Scriptures also imply that there is an organizational hierarchy of angels. What biblical authors present this idea? (pp. 77–79)

3. Though believers have held various opinions about the categories and ranking of angels since the time of the early church fathers, it seems clear from the Bible that there are different _____ of angels and that angels have various _____ in God's kingdom. (p. 79)

4. Who is the only archangel mentioned by name in the Bible? What is his main role? What should the character of this archangel inspire in us? (pp. 80, 82–83)

5. Who is another angel who plays a prominent role in Scripture and may also be an archangel? What is his main role? What should his character inspire in us? (pp. 83, 87–88)

6. What two special kinds of angels are prominent in the Bible? (p. 88)

7. Describe the contemporary culture's idea of a cherub. (p. 88)

8. What are biblical cherubim really like? What is their role? (pp. 88–93)

245

9. Which cherub rebelled against God and fell from his position in heaven? What can his fall teach us? (p. 93)

10. What are seraphim like? What is their role? (pp. 94–96)

11. What can we learn from the seraphim that we can apply to our own relationships with God? (p. 96)

12. What does the term "angel of the Lord" or "Angel of the Lord" refer to? (p. 96)

Chapter Five: Ministering Spirits

1. What is the primary role of all angels? (p. 99)

2. What is a second major role of angels? (p. 101)

3. Name the Scripture verse that tells us angels minister to those who have received eternal life in Christ. (p. 101)

4. List eight ways in which God's angels minister to His people. (pp. 102–120)

5. How does the author define "defensive" and "offensive" angels? (p. 116)

6. What is a third major role of angels? (p. 120)

7. Describe a fourth major role of angels. (p. 123)

8. What are three aspects of this fourth role? (pp. 123–24)

9. How has this chapter's emphasis on God's ministering angels changed your perspective on your relationship with God and your ministry/service for Him?

Chapter Six: Angels and Protection

1. Angels are our spiritual _____. (p. 133)

2. Psalm 91 gives several reasons God's people are protected. What are those reasons? (pp. 133–34)

3. What does Mary Baxter urge parents to do on behalf of their children, and why? (p. 135)

4. What was the reason the author prayed for her son at the particular time that she did? (p. 134)

5. Why did she pray when, at the time, she didn't fully know what her prayers were for? (p. 134)

6. Have you ever been prompted by the Holy Spirit to pray for a person or situation without fully knowing the circumstances? How did you respond? Did you ever learn the reason you were prompted to pray? If so, what were the circumstances? What did you learn from this experience?

7. Mary Baxter talked about how she is protected by angels as she is ministering. (p. 138) How could knowing about God's protecting angels give you courage to tell others about the Gospel—even under difficult circumstances?

8. How does the author define the "blood covering" or "blood covenant"? (pp. 140–41)

9. What does it mean for us to dedicate someone or something to the Father, the Son, and the Holy Spirit? (p. 141)

10. What have you learned about God's protection of yourself and others based on what you have read in this chapter?

Chapter Seven: Angels and God's Word

1. In Mary Baxter's visions of the pulpits on fire, what was the fire meant to signify? What did God evidently tell the author happens when His Word is preached? (pp. 145–47)

2. What does it mean to "rebuild the altars of God"? (p. 148)

3. How are we to clean the altars of our hearts and make them altars to God? (pp. 149–51)

4. What was the vision of the glory and power intermingling with fire meant to convey? (p. 154)

5. What are two biblical promises that we can include in our prayers for the salvation of our loved ones? (p. 154)

6. What effect does the Word of God have on Satan? (p. 155)

7. What are two verses that assure us of the effectiveness of God's Word? (p. 158)

8. Have you been reading, meditating on, memorizing, believing, applying, and obeying the Word of God? In what ways?

9. What specific steps can you take to become more committed to God and His Word? What difference will this make in your life?

10. How will you apply God's Word and faith in Him to a difficult situation or personal struggle in your life today?

Chapter Eight: Angels and God's Fire

1. God's fire accomplishes what two things? (p. 161)

2. What does it mean to *"purge out the old leaven"* (1 Corinthians 5:7)? (p. 163)

3. Why do people sometimes feel heat when they are healed by the Lord? (p. 164)

4. What was the meaning of the plumb line in the Lord's hand in Amos 7:7–8? (p. 165)

5. According to Isaiah 28:17, what criteria of measurement does God use when measuring our lives? (p. 165)

6. Mary Baxter says she believes God's judgment is with us today and that He is setting a "plumb line" among us. How should we respond to this judgment? (pp. 165–67)

7. What can happen when we resist conviction of sin in our lives? (p. 167)

8. What are two consequences of falling into sin and dishonesty before God? (p. 167)

9. Jesus was manifested to _____ us from sin and _____ us from eternal punishment. We serve a mighty God who _____ and _____ _____ us. (p. 168)

10. How do you usually respond to God's discipline and correction? Do you ignore or fight it? Or do you allow God to renew and cleanse you through His forgiveness, His Spirit, and His Word?

11. What specific steps should you take to yield to God's loving discipline when He convicts you of sin or a lack of devotion to Him? (See 1 John 1:7–8; Psalm 119:9–11; Galatians 5:16.)

12. Is the Holy Spirit convicting you of something today? How will you respond?

Chapter Nine: Angels and Deliverance

1. When we are in right relationship with God, what two things happen as we *call upon [the Lord] in the day of trouble* (Psalm 50:15)? (p. 169)

2. In this chapter, the author mentions several things that bring about deliverance, healing, and salvation. What are they? (pp. 172–78)

3. How did the author's understanding of Jesus' sufferings and sacrifice of atonement affect the way she looked at her painful circumstances? How can it affect the way you see your own difficult situations? (p. 178)

4. Once a person has been delivered by the power of God, what needs to happen in order for him to *stay* delivered? (pp. 187–88)

5. Another aspect of deliverance is provided in Isaiah 10:27, which says, *"The yoke shall be destroyed because of the _____ "* (KJV). (p. 189)

6. What are two things a person should do to be set free from the yoke of bondage? (pp. 189–90)

7. What did Mary Baxter say had to happen first in the country that worshiped false gods and idols before its people could be open to receive the Gospel? (pp. 190–92)

8. The devil has to back off and release his victims when he is cast out in the _____ of Jesus. (p. 193)

9. What should we have before we cast out Satan and his demons in this way? (p. 193)

10. For what reasons does God *always* have the victory over Satan? (pp. 194–95)

11. Based on what you have learned in this chapter, what areas of your own life or the lives of your friends and loved ones need to be addressed before you or they can receive deliverance? (For example, do you need to forgive someone who has wronged you? Do you need to ask Christ to fill you with His compassion for others? Are you being open and honest before God and seeking to live according to His Word? Are you interceding for others so that they can be set free from Satan's control and be able to hear the Gospel?) What will you do today to begin to address an area you need to deal with so that deliverance can come?

12. Build your faith in God's deliverance by memorizing and meditating on Scriptures such as the following:

And the Lord will deliver me from every evil work and preserve me for His heavenly kingdom. (2 Timothy 4:18)

*The Lord knows how to deliver the godly
out of temptations.*   (2 Peter 2:9)

*The angel of the LORD encamps all around
those who fear Him, and delivers them.*
(Psalm 34:7)

*Blessed is he who considers the poor; the
LORD will deliver him in time of trouble.
The LORD will preserve him and keep him
alive, and he will be blessed on the earth;
You will not deliver him to the will of his
enemies. The LORD will strengthen him
on his bed of illness; You will sustain him
on his sickbed.*   (Psalm 41:1–3)

Chapter Ten: Angels and Prayer

1. On what basis can we join with the angels
   in worshiping God? What sacrifices do
   we need to offer God in worship? (p. 201)

2. According to Revelation 8:3–4, what happens to the prayers of the saints? (p.
   201–2)

3. What are four types of prayers that the angels help answer? (pp. 202, 205, 210–11)

4. In what four ways did Mary Baxter say that God taught her to pray for people's deliverance? (p. 219)

5. When should believers pray? (p. 220)

6. How important to God are the prayers of believers? (pp. 220–21)

7. What have you learned from this chapter about the effect that believers' prayers can have on salvation, healing, miracles, and deliverance?

8. How seriously have you taken the role of your prayers for the fulfillment of God's purposes in the world?

9. What specific steps will you take to develop your prayer life and intercede on behalf of others who need God's forgiveness, wholeness, and deliverance?

Chapter Eleven: The Meaning of Angels

1. How can the study of angels help us spiritually? (pp. 223–24)

2. What are we to focus on as we learn about angels? (p. 223)

3. God has angels for every _____ you have. (p. 224)

4. The Word of God and the angels are always in _____ accomplishing His _____. (p. 224)

5. God wants us to participate with Him in fulfilling His purposes. List six important truths for loving and serving God that should be a part of our lives as we help fulfill His will. (pp. 224–27, 233–34)

6. Angels are an example to us of how we should _____ and worship God. (pp. 224–25)

7. What should learning about the ministry of angels on our behalf do for our faith? (p. 225)

8. As we trust God in all things and for all things, what should we concentrate on? (p. 226)

9. What two things should we be doing to discern false angelic beings or evil spirits? (p. 227)

10. Question number 4 of the first chapter asked if you (or someone you know) had experienced what you considered an angelic visitation. (See page 240.) After reading this book and working through the questions in this section, how would you now define that encounter? Do you think it was a true angel or a false angelic being? What is your reason for thinking this?

11. The faces at the ends of the ropes in Mary Baxter's vision signified mercy and truth. God says we must have both of these qualities in our lives in order to be like Him. How can mercy and truth meet together in our hearts? (pp. 229–30)

12. We can be obedient to God only as we abide in Christ and honor His Word in our lives. [See John 15:5–8.] (p. 231) Are you abiding in Christ, or have you drifted away from your Source of spiritual life? What will you do today to join yourself to, or remain connected to, the Vine, Jesus Christ?

13. Through what two things does Hebrews 6:12 tell us we can inherit the promises of God? (p. 233)

14. How does the Holy Spirit help us in our prayers? [See Romans 8:26–27.] (p. 234)

15. God is the God of both _____ and _____. (p. 235)

Answer Key

Chapter One: Are Angels Real?

1. Answers will vary.

2. Answers will vary.

3. Answers will vary.

4. Answers will vary.

5. Mary Baxter says she was given visions and revelations so she could give them to the body of Christ and those who are not yet believers; they are signs that God is working among His people. The revelations are also meant to bring Him honor and glory and to draw people close to Him. God wants to give people hope and encouragement, to show them that He loves them and is with them, and to bring them salvation, healing, and deliverance.

Chapter Two: The Truth about Angels

1. (a) Much of so-called teaching on angels making the rounds these days—even in religious circles—is false, and it causes people to be deceived. In addition, not all angels are holy and good. Evil angels seek to deceive us about their true intentions toward us. They are demons that want to harm us rather than help us. We have to understand the truth about God's angels if we are going to be able to discern what is counterfeit. (b) The

Bible is God's own Word and is completely trust-worthy.

2. Angels are not divine; they were created by God to minister to Him. True angels never accept worship from human beings; they are co-worshipers and fellow servants of God with us. Angels do God's bidding, not their own or ours. Praying directly to an angel may open a person up to spiritual deception because the "angel" may actually be an evil spirit disguised as an angel of light. (See 2 Corinthians 11:14.)

3. God alone, because He is the One who sends and empowers the angels who help us.

4. Jesus Christ is God, and He created the angels. When He came to earth as a man, He temporarily set aside the splendor, but not the reality, of His deity. In this way, He became *"a little lower than the angels"* (Psalm 8:5) for a time in order to secure our salvation by dying for our sins on the cross and rising again in victory. When He ascended to heaven, God put all things in heaven and earth under His authority—including all the angels, all humanity, and Satan and his demons.

5. Angels were created before mankind, and throughout the Word of God, they are depicted as existing on a level somewhere between God and man. Angels and people are always distinct creations; human beings do not become angels when they die. Angels are a higher form of creation than

humans in the sense that, right now, they have higher spiritual knowledge, power, and mobility. In addition, God's holy angels never sin against Him. As long as we are on earth and not yet totally free from our tendency to sin, then we are not as morally good as God's holy angels. Yet humanity will ultimately be elevated higher than the angels. God sent His Son to earth to die for us when mankind fell. (He didn't do that for the angels who fell and rebelled against Him.) We are redeemed through the blood of Christ, and we have the righteousness of Jesus Himself. This gives us a high and exalted position with God. Paul wrote of the time after Jesus comes back when Christians will exist in a glorified state. (See Romans 8:18, 30.) At that time, we will be higher than the angels, and we will even judge them (1 Corinthians 6:3).

6. The Bible instructs us to try or test the spirits to see if they are authentic: *"Every spirit that confesses ["acknowledges" NIV] that Jesus Christ has come in the flesh is of God, and every spirit that does not confess ["acknowledge" NIV] that Jesus Christ has come in the flesh is not of God"* (1 John 4:2–3). If a spiritual being communicates any message that denies the deity, humanity, and salvation of the Lord Jesus, it is not from God. If its message promotes an unscriptural message or practice, if it draws attention to itself rather than Jesus, then that spirit being is a demon attempting to deceive people. We should continually read

and meditate on God's Word in order to be able to discern the spirits.

7. Your ultimate protection against the enemy's deception and evil is to believe in the Lord Jesus Christ and to receive Him as your Savior. Jesus will be faithful to forgive you and cleanse you completely, and you will be kept by His power. He will give you the gift of the Holy Spirit, who will live within you and enable you to obey and serve God. You will become a part of God's own family, and His angels will watch over you. In addition, as you study about angels, you should pray to God the Father, in Jesus' name, and ask for His direction and protection so that you will not be deceived by the enemy.

Chapter Three: What Are Angels Like?

1. Angels are (1) spirit beings, (2) holy, (3) elect, (4) intelligent, but not omniscient, (5) powerful, but not omnipotent.

2. Spirits are immortal, are not subject to physical limitations of time or space, and have no gender (they do not marry or have children).

3. Angels know only what God chooses to reveal to them or allows them to know. The Bible teaches that angels learn things by observing God's working in and through His people. Paul wrote about how God uses the church to reveal certain things to His holy angels. (See 1 Corinthians 4:9; Ephesians 3:8–10.)

4. (At least) more than one hundred million, and likely more than we can count. (See Revelation 5:11; Hebrews 12:22.)

5. In the Bible, angels appeared to humanity in (1) shining or dazzling appearance, (2) strange forms or features, and (3) human form.

6. Answers may vary from the examples given on pp. 66–72.

7. Hebrews 13:2 says, *"Do not forget to entertain strangers, for by so doing some people have entertained angels without knowing it"* (NIV). We are told to be hospitable to strangers because they just might be angels disguised as humans. In addition, God wants us to love and serve Him not only in the obvious presence of His holy angels, but also in the presence of human beings, who are precious in His sight. The Bible exhorts us in 1 John 4:20, *"If someone says, 'I love God,' and hates his brother, he is a liar; for he who does not love his brother whom he has seen, how can he love God whom he has not seen?"*

Chapter Four: Types and Ranks of Angels

1. angels, archangels, cherubim, and seraphim

2. Matthew quoted Jesus' reference to *"legions of angels"* (26:53). Jude mentioned the archangel Michael (v. 9). Paul spoke of *"the voice of an archangel"* (1 Thessalonians 4:16) and gave a glimpse into the organization of angels in various other

passages in his letters. (See Romans 8:38–39; Ephesians 1:20–22; 3:9–10; Colossians 1:16.)

3. types; positions

4. Michael is the only archangel the Scriptures mention by name. He is always depicted in the Bible in spiritual conflict with evil and wicked powers, and he appears to be the supreme commander of the angels who do warfare for God—the "hosts" of heaven. Michael should be an inspiration to us to be faithful and obedient to God as we serve His purposes in His kingdom.

5. Gabriel is another angel who plays a prominent role in Scripture and may also be an archangel. This angel's appearance in the Bible always seems related to the mission of announcing to God's people His purpose and program concerning Jesus the Messiah and "the time of the end." Gabriel's reverence for God, His Word, and His work should inspire us to love and serve God as He carries out His purposes in our own lives and in the lives of all humanity.

6. cherubim and seraphim

7. Contemporary society's idea of cherubs is that of plump little babies with wings.

8. Cherubim are powerful and holy beings who are closely associated with God, His purity, and His glory. Ezekiel 10:1–21 describes their features in detail, including their backs, wings, hands of a man, and wheels—all of which are full of eyes.

Each also has four faces: the face of a cherub, the face of a man, the face of a lion, and the face of an eagle.

9. Lucifer, or the devil, was the cherub who rebelled against God. Lucifer's fall is a grave reminder to us of the consequences of sin, if even a cherub can have such an end. Yet it is also a reminder of the great sacrifice of Christ on our behalf that restores us to the very presence of God as if we had never sinned. As Hebrews 2:16 says, *"For indeed He does not give aid to angels, but He does give aid to the seed of Abraham."*

10. Seraphim hover above God's throne and are closer than all the other angels to their Creator. In Isaiah 6:1–4, the seraphim are described as powerful beings who have six wings and who give reverent praise to God for His holiness and glory; they seem to dwell in the midst of God's holiness. Of the seraphim's six wings, two pairs cover their faces and feet in the presence of God's brilliant glory, while only one pair is used for flying.

11. Seraphim are intelligent beings who celebrate the Holy One. They are aflame with love for God. Their devotion should inspire deep love for God in us, as well.

12. At various times, the biblical term "angel of the Lord" or "Angel of the Lord" may be referring to one of God's angels, to God Himself, or to the Lord Jesus Christ in what is often called a pre-incarnate appearance.

Chapter Five: Ministering Spirits

1. The primary role of all angels is to praise and exalt God and His Son, Jesus Christ.

2. Angels are also God's willing servants. They are His active agents who do His will day and night as they minister to Him and His people.

3. Hebrews 1:14 says, *"Are not all angels ministering spirits sent to serve those who will inherit salvation?"* (NIV).

4. Angels (1) bring special messages from God; (2) deliver God's Word to people and also help them to understand it; (3) bring God's guidance, directing people's steps and clearing the path before them as they do His will; (4) comfort and encourage people during difficult times in their lives; (5) strengthen and sustain God's people; (6) protect and deliver believers; (7) promote the Gospel; and (8) convey the souls of God's people to heaven.

5. Defensive angels protect us from harm and danger and all kinds of evil devices of Satan. They serve as guardian angels. They protect us even when we don't know they are there. Offensive angels wage active war against strongholds, principalities, demons, forces of darkness, and everything else that opposes the work of God.

6. Angels defend God's honor and glory; they help fight His battles and execute His judgments in the world.

7. Angels will participate in end-time events. They will help bring this world to a culmination as the old heavens and earth pass away and the new heavens and earth come into being.

8. Angels will, first of all, accompany Jesus when He returns to the earth. Second, angels will harvest the disobedient for the Day of Judgment. Third, angels will gather together all the righteous for eternal life.

9. Answers will vary.

Chapter Six: Angels and Protection

1. guardians

2. Psalm 91 says, *"**Because you have made the LORD, who is my refuge, even the Most High, your dwelling place**, no evil shall befall you, nor shall any plague come near your dwelling....*[The Lord says,] *"**Because he has set his love upon Me**, therefore I will deliver him; I will set him on high, **because he has known My name**. He shall call upon Me, and I will answer him; I will be with him in trouble; I will deliver him and honor him. With long life I will satisfy him, and show him My salvation"* (vv. 9–10, 14–16, emphasis added).

3. Mary Baxter says parents need to "press into God in prayer" for their children because, many times, the children's safety may depend on their parents' prayers for protection.

4. The Holy Spirit prompted the author to intercede in a special way while she was praying, and she began to pray earnestly in the Spirit.

5. The wording of answers will vary, but should be similar to the following: Although Mary Baxter didn't understand all of what she was praying, only a part of it, she trusted in the leading of the Holy Spirit and responded immediately to His prompting.

6. Answers will vary.

7. The wording of answers will vary, but should be similar to the following: Knowing that God is taking care of us, that His protecting angels are nearby, and that nothing can happen to us that He does not allow can give us courage to speak the truth of the Gospel, even though there may be opposition, rejection of the message, and even persecution.

8. Our salvation in Christ includes the protective covering of the precious blood He shed on the cross when He became our Substitute. When we pray for people, and God impresses upon us to cover people with the blood, we should say, "I cover you with the blood of Jesus, the covenant of God!" This means that Jesus Christ is the Son of God who was sent from heaven. He knew His purpose and His destiny. He was sent to give His life on a cruel cross for you and me, so that we could have eternal life. He died so that our sins could be washed away. When we

pray or command a covering of His blood, we are affirming that we believe Jesus provided a covering for us and our families through the Atonement. The angels go to us immediately and seal and protect us. Through the blood covenant, we build a hedge of protection around our families and ourselves.

9. When we sincerely dedicate someone or something to the Father, the Son, and the Holy Spirit and anoint the person or thing with oil, we are saying, "This is God's territory." When spiritual enemies try to come, they have to back up because that "territory" has been dedicated to God.

10. Answers will vary.

Chapter Seven: Angels and God's Word

1. The fire represented pulpits where God's true Word was being preached, where those who preached revered and honored God, wanted things *"done decently and in order"* (1 Corinthians 14:40), and exhibited the love of Christ. When God's Word is preached, His people are purified, and His Spirit is with His ministers to bring deliverance and the fulfillment of His Word in people's lives.

2. To "rebuild the altars of God" means to preach the truth and walk in God's ways.

3. We are to acknowledge that God is holy and righteous; tell Him the truth about our lives, confessing our sins so He can set us free through Christ; repent of our ungodly ways; and make a

new commitment to Him. When we do this, He will purify and deliver us.

4. It was meant to convey that, what God has said in His Word, He *will* accomplish.

5. *"Great shall be the peace of your children"* (Isaiah 54:13). *"[God] will also bless the fruit of your womb"* (Deuteronomy 7:13).

6. God's Word is *"the sword of the Spirit"* (Ephesians 6:17) and defeats the enemy.

7. Ezekiel 12:25 says, *"For I am the LORD. I speak, and the word which I speak will come to pass."* Hebrews 4:12 says, *"For the word of God is living and powerful, and sharper than any two-edged sword, piercing even to the division of soul and spirit, and of joints and marrow, and is a discerner of the thoughts and intents of the heart."*

8. Answers will vary.

9. Answers will vary.

10. Answers will vary.

Chapter Eight: Angels and God's Fire

1. God's fire is a fire of 1) revival, purification, and healing for His people, and (2) judgment for those who reject Him.

2. It means to remove sin and disobedience from our lives and allow the character and Spirit of Christ to rule in our hearts.

3. They are feeling fire or heat from the power of God, which is "burning out" their diseases and sicknesses.

4. The plumb line was a symbolic way of indicating that God was measuring the lives of the Israelites to see if they were spiritually upright.

5. justice and righteousness: *"I will make justice the measuring line, and righteousness the* [plumb line]" (Isaiah 28:17).

6. We need to be devoted to God with all our hearts. He does not want people to experience judgment but to repent and turn to Him through Christ before it is too late. We cannot allow the devil to distract us from hearing and obeying the truth. Our lives can be measured as righteous only as we receive the Lord Jesus Christ and His righteousness through the atonement He provided for us when He died on the cross, and as we remain in His righteousness through faith and obedience to Him. We are not to take sin lightly. We should allow God to purge us with His fire and to cleanse us by His holy Word so we will be prepared for the coming of the Lord.

7. We can begin to harden our hearts against God.

8. First, moving away from the righteousness and holiness of Christ causes openings to be created in our spiritual hedge of protection. Second, openings are also created in our anointing from

God, and, pretty soon, we become corrupt, with the enemy attacking us every way he can. We can then become filled with lies and sin.

9. deliver; save; loves; cares about

10. Answers will vary.

11. Answers will vary, but should include the following: Admit my sin to God, confess and repent of my sins, and receive God's forgiveness and cleansing through Christ. Commit to living according to God's Word, seek God with all my heart, and hide God's Word in my heart (memorizing, meditating on, and treasuring His Word). Finally, walk according to God's Spirit and ways.

12. Answers will vary.

Chapter Nine: Angels and Deliverance

1. God will deliver us, and we will glorify Him (Psalm 50:15).

2. God's presence, the power of the Cross (what Jesus accomplished for us in the Atonement), and God's compassion.

3. The author gained even greater respect for what Jesus went through and for the love God showed us in sending His Son Jesus to give us eternal life. She realized that, while we are on this earth, we have to continue to tear down Satan's kingdom through the Word of God. We have to continue to do the things that God would have us to do. The vision also gave her unbelievable joy. Through it, God encouraged her

and reminded her that *"surely He has borne our griefs and carried our sorrows"* (Isaiah 53:4). He assured her that her relatives could be set free. *"Believe on the Lord Jesus Christ, and you will be saved, you and your household"* (Acts 16:31).

4. First, those who are ministering to the person have to continue to pray for him. They also have to counsel him, teaching him that, after a person is delivered, he can't be involved any longer with the things that bound him in the first place. Second, the person seeking deliverance can't be double-minded about it. He has to decide if he really wants to adore Jesus and serve Him, or if he wants to follow the things of the world and the devil. If the person wants to taste the goodness of God and the world at the same time, there is a fatal conflict in his heart that has to be resolved. He needs to find a good church that believes in Jesus Christ and His deliverance. Next, he must obey the Word of God. He also needs to keep away from sinful things that drag him down. In addition, he should stay close to the heart of God. The person should worship, serve, and praise God, and, through every situation, trust that God will give him the victory.

5. anointing

6. First, the person must stay honest in his soul before God, repenting of his sins and asking God to forgive and help him. Second, he must be sure to forgive other people for any wrongs they have

committed against him. The Word of God says we must forgive anyone who has harmed or hurt us so that the heavenly Father will forgive us. Jesus said in Matthew 6:14–15, *"For if you forgive men their trespasses, your heavenly Father will also forgive you. But if you do not forgive men their trespasses, neither will your Father forgive your trespasses."*

7. God first sent His angels to deliver that country from the demon of idolatry and from the worship of idols because of the earnest prayers of His people. This enabled the eyes and ears of the citizens of that nation to be open the Gospel so they could receive salvation.

8. name

9. We must have a genuine relationship with the Lord so that we use His name with true reverence and faith.

10. First, Satan is only a created being, while God is divine and eternal. The devil is neither omnipotent, omniscient, nor omnipresent, as God is. Second, the Lord Jesus Christ is always stronger than the devil or any of his demons. The Bible says He *"has gone into heaven and is at the right hand of God, angels and authorities and powers having been made subject to Him"* (1 Peter 3:22). In addition, God has multitudes of angels to carry out His works and plans. Regardless of how many demons the devil has, God's holy angels are more in number.

11. Answers will vary.

Chapter Ten: Angels and Prayer

1. We can worship God because of Jesus' sacrifice on the cross, through which He has reconciled us to God and restored our relationship with Him. In addition, worship is possible only as we offer the Lord our own sacrifices—sacrifices of praise.

2. The prayers of the saints are offered by an angel along with incense on the altar of heaven that is before the throne of God. This mixture of prayers and incense ascends before Him.

3. The angels help answer prayers for (1) salvation, (2) healing, (3) miracles, and (4) deliverance.

4. Mary Baxter was taught (1) how to pray through the Scriptures, (2) how to bind and loose (see Matthew 18:18), (3) how to plead the precious blood of Jesus, and (4) how to rely on the Word of God.

5. We shouldn't pray just once a day and then forget about it. When the Holy Spirit prompts us to pray, we should pray right then, regardless of where we are. In addition, the apostle Paul taught believers to *"pray without ceasing"* (1 Thessalonians 5:17) in the Spirit.

6. The prayers of believers are very important to God. Through the prayers of those who believe His Word, God commissions His angels to come

and work with us, and He brings salvation, healing, and deliverance to people.

7. Answers will vary.

8. Answers will vary.

9. Answers will vary.

Chapter Eleven: The Meaning of Angels

1. The study of angels provides us with a wonderful opportunity to come to know God and His ways better. In addition, our knowledge of God's special messengers and how He works through them can help to enlighten our doubts, solidify our beliefs, comfort us in sorrow, and give us peace. The ministry of angels on our behalf reveals that God loves us and is continually working to help us. This knowledge can bring us comfort and joy.

2. As we learn about angels, we are not to place our focus on celestial beings themselves but on almighty God and the power and grace He manifests through His servants, the angels.

3. need

4. action; purposes

5. Six truths for loving and serving God are the importance of (1) worship, (2) believing, (3) discernment, (4) obedience, (5) perseverance, and (6) prayer.

6. reverence

7. Learning about the ministry of angels on our behalf should give us confidence in God's love

and power, and encourage our hearts that God is with us, no matter what we're going through.

8. We should concentrate on loving and serving God.

9. We must fill our hearts and minds with God's Word and test the spirits. (See 1 John 4:1–3.)

10. Answers will vary.

11. Mercy and truth will meet together in our hearts when we worship God in *"spirit and truth"* (John 4:23–24), when we love God with all our hearts, souls, strength, and minds (Luke 10:27), and when we yield to God and live a holy life— body, mind, and spirit. (See 1 Thessalonians 5:23.)

12. Answers will vary.

13. faith and patience

14. Romans 8:26–27 says that when we do not know how to pray for someone or something, the Holy Spirit intercedes for us with deep groans that cannot be expressed in human terms, but which God understands. The Spirit prays for the saints according to the will of God.

15. angels; men

About the Author

Mary Katherine Baxter was born in Chattanooga, Tennessee. While she was still young, her mother taught her about Jesus Christ and His salvation. At the age of nineteen, she was born again.

In 1976, while she was living in Belleville, Michigan, Jesus appeared to her in human form, as well as in visions and revelations. During those visits, He revealed to her the depths, degrees, levels, and torments of lost souls in hell, telling her that this message is for the whole world. Since that time, she has received many visitations from the Lord. In God's wisdom, to give balance to her message, she has also received many visions, dreams, and revelations of heaven, angels, and the end of time.

On Mary's tours of hell, she walked with Jesus and talked with many people. Jesus showed her what happens to unrepentant souls when they die and what happens to servants of God when they do not remain obedient to their calling, go back into a life of sin, and refuse to repent.

Mary was ordained as a minister in 1983 at a Full Gospel church in Taylor, Michigan. Ministers, leaders, and saints of the Lord around the world speak very highly of her and her ministry. The movement of the Holy Spirit is emphasized in all her services, and many miracles have occurred in them. The gifts of the Holy Spirit with demonstrations of power are manifested in her meetings as the Spirit of God leads and empowers her.

Mary loves the Lord with everything she has—all her heart, mind, soul, and strength. She is truly a dedicated handmaiden of the Lord, and she desires above all to be a soulwinner for Jesus Christ. From the headquarters of Divine Revelation, Inc., her Florida-based ministry, this anointed evangelist continues to travel the world, telling her story of heaven and hell and her revelatory visits from the Lord.

For speaking engagements, please contact:

Evangelist Mary K. Baxter
Divine Revelation, Inc.
P.O. Box 121524
West Melbourne, FL 32912-1524
e-mail: marybaxter@live.com
www.mbaxterdivinerevelation.org

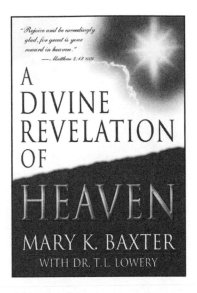

A Divine Revelation of Heaven

Mary K. Baxter
with Dr. T. L. Lowery

After thirty nights of experiencing the depths of hell, best-selling author Mary Baxter was shown the realms of heaven. Included in these fascinating pages are her descriptions of the order of heaven, what happens to children after death, angels at work, and the throne of God. These breathtaking glimpses of heaven will turn your heart toward the beauty and joy that await every believer in Christ.

ISBN: 978-0-88368-524-2 • Trade • 208 pages

WHITAKER
HOUSE

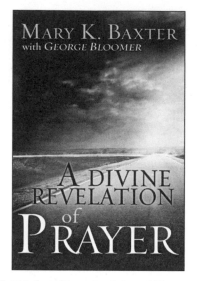

A Divine Revelation of Prayer
Mary K. Baxter
with George Bloomer

Many Christians question why they can't overcome sin and temptation and why they don't get answers to their prayers for improved health, financial blessings, and better relationships. Best-selling author Mary K. Baxter shares eye-opening visions and revelations on the power of prayer. Her remarkable personal answers to prayer will help you overcome fears and failures, receive healing and freedom from addictions, discern clear direction from God, and experience His divine power daily. Discover the keys to life-changing breakthroughs in prayer today!

ISBN: 978-1-60374-050-0 • Trade • 256 pages

WHITAKER
HOUSE